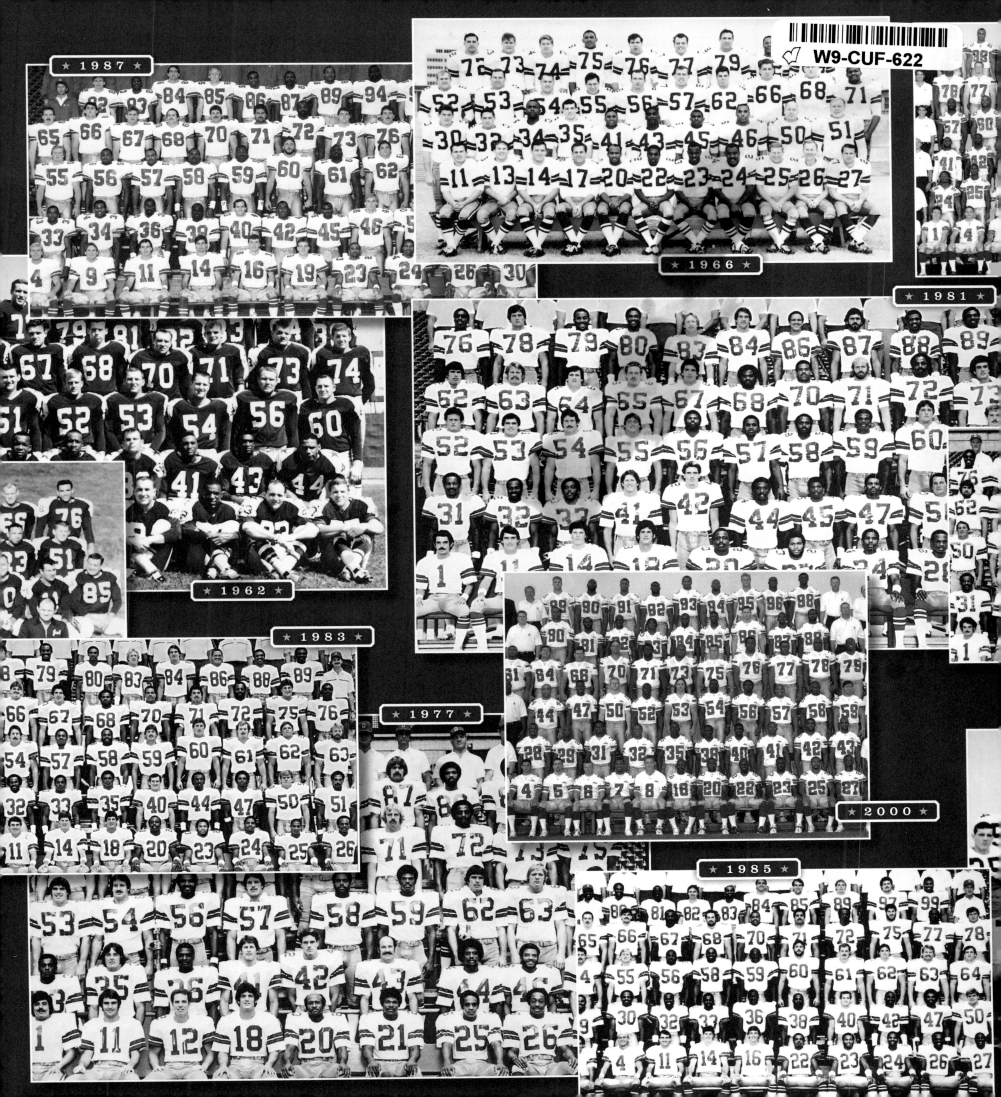

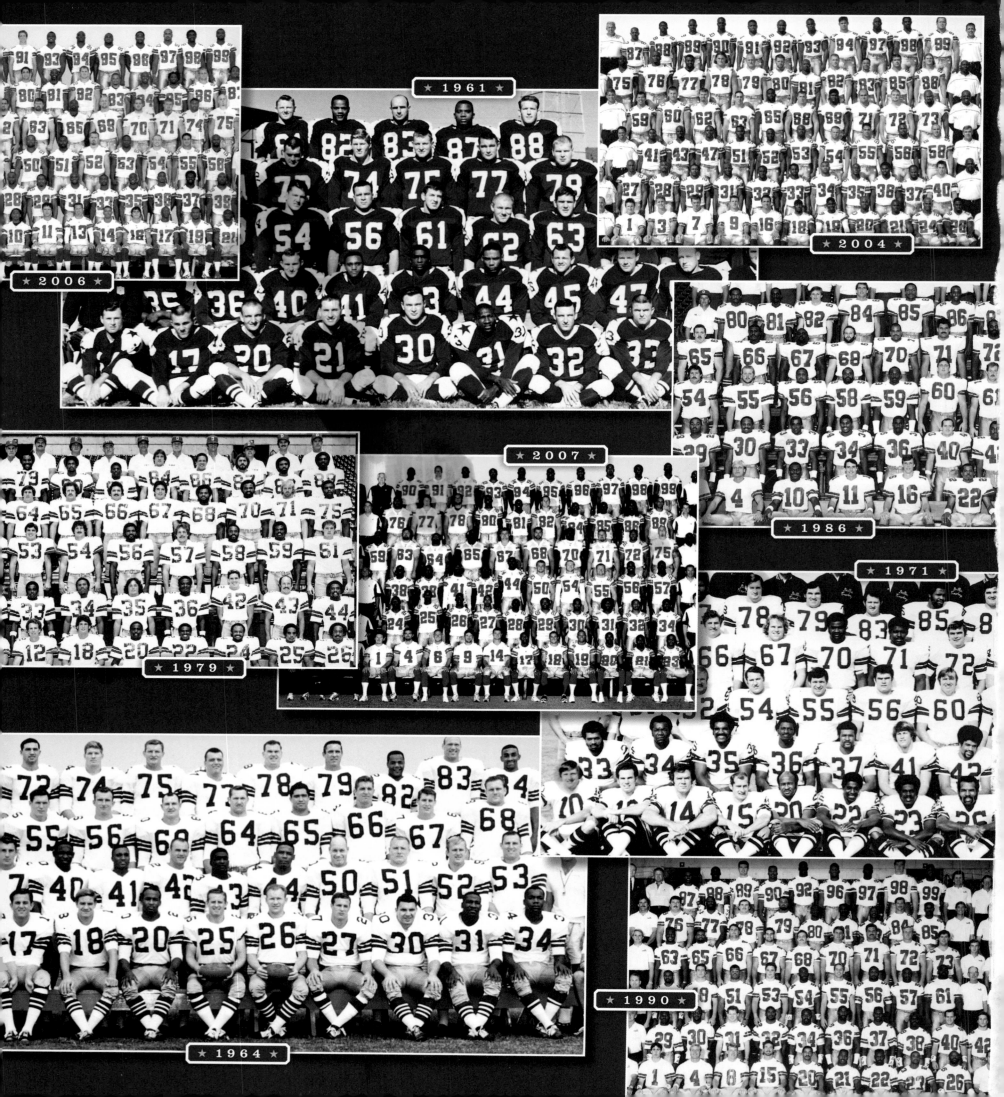

Dallas
COWBOYS

★ *Receiver Billy Howton's 1960 helmet bore the original Cowboy star.*

Sports Illustrated

Dallas
COWBOYS

50 YEARS OF FOOTBALL

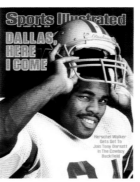
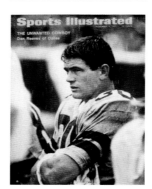

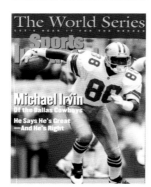
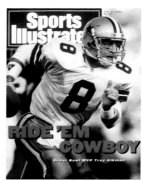

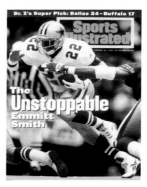

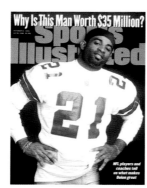
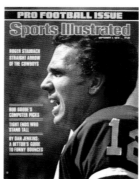

★ CONTENTS ★

EDITOR
David Bauer

ART DIRECTOR
Steven Hoffman

PHOTO EDITOR
Cristina Scalet

COPY EDITOR
Kevin Kerr

ASSOCIATE
EDITOR
David Sabino

DESIGNER
Josh Denkin

REPORTER
Adam Duerson

PROJECT
MANAGER
Stefanie Kaufman

★ *Safety Dick Daniels (21), a sub, and receiver Bob Hayes, a star, were equally cold as they huddled during the frigid "Ice Bowl" in Green Bay in 1967.*

THE COWBOYS MATTER MORE

A FOOTBALL CONVERT LEARNS TO APPRECIATE THAT TEAM IN DALLAS

BY PETER KING

THIS IS GOING TO SOUND FAWNING, I know, but it's not: Where would we be without the Dallas Cowboys? Or let me ask it this way: Where would *I* be without the Cowboys? ★ I grew up in Connecticut, a New York Giants fan, hating the Cowboys. In the mid-1960s, the Dallas team was still in its infancy, but from the time I first started watching football, the Cowboys were the Giants' rival I most vividly recollect. Those were the Cowboys teams I hated. The first football game I can specifically recall watching on TV was the now-famous Ice Bowl in Green Bay in '67, with the flickering images of frozen men on the black-and-white set in our living room. I was 10. What did I care, really, about this game between the Packers and Cowboys half a country away? Yet I desperately wanted the Cowboys to lose. I know now that Tom Landry and Bob Lilly were honorable men, but not on that day, not to me. It was this way: If my Giants and my

★ *The Super Bowl XXX ring consecrates the Cowboys fifth title, a 27–17 win over the Steelers.*

★ SUPER BOWL XXVIII: *Cowboys 30, Bills 13* ★

★ SUPER BOWL XXVII: *Cowboys 52, Bills 17* ★

Red Sox couldn't win, then I was damn sure going to root for the despised Cowboys and the dreaded Yankees to lose.

Later, in high school, I drove an hour down to the Yale Bowl in New Haven, where the Giants played in 1974 while a new stadium was being built. There, to my great dismay, I saw Roger Staubach throw a touchdown pass to Drew Pearson and Dallas win easily, 21–7. I went to college in Ohio; still a Giants fan, I had to fight off the two annoying Cowboys fans in my dorm for the TV in the basement whenever a Dallas game was on. I met a girl at school and went to Pittsburgh to meet her family—and the whole family hated the Cowboys too. Ha! Never, ever, in that house were they called the Cowboys. Always the Cryboys, a team whining to the league office to get its way. My future father-in-law thought Tex Schramm had commissioner Pete Rozelle wrapped around his finger, and that every time there was a controversial call, it would go the Cowboys' way. And why try to convince him otherwise? His rants made for such great entertainment.

In the '70s, the Steelers won, the Dolphins won, the Raiders won. And the Cowboys won—but somehow there was a difference. Somehow, the Cowboys always mattered more. Not just to me, to everybody. I had to admit it: Hate them or love them, they just mattered more.

When I began covering the Giants in 1985 for a New York paper, *Newsday*, my love-the-Giants-hate-the-Cowboys heritage disappeared in about two weeks. I began rooting for stories, not for a team. Bill Parcells, the Giants coach at the time, couldn't understand that. He thought I was a subversive.

By the time I got to SPORTS ILLUSTRATED in 1989, the Cowboys had struggled through the late '80s and I started covering the team's renaissance under Jerry Jones and Jimmy Johnson. My editor had two rules when it came to football coverage. One: stars, stars, stars. You can never go wrong writing about stars. Two: When in doubt, write about the Cowboys. "For some reason," he used to say, "America cares about the Cowboys whether they're hot or they're cold."

It was true. Covering the league for SI, I could never get enough of Dallas; every time I was around the Cowboys, it felt like a big story. And it was always interesting. Very interesting.

Like the time in 1990 when a young Michael Irvin, relishing his interview with SI, said to me, "Let's go to my office. Follow me there." He got in his car, I in mine, and before long we arrived at a strip club, complete with, you know, strip-club activities. His office. I interviewed him at a table there for some 45 minutes; he was thoughtful and expansive, seemingly oblivious to the G-strings and flesh all around.

Or the time the next year when Jimmy Johnson let me accompany the coaches on a three-city scouting trip before the draft. At Tennessee, the Dallas coaching staff drank with Vols head coach Johnny Majors till the wee hours, and I found out exactly how the Cowboys learned the deep, dark secrets about players. I remember thinking how successful Johnson was going to be, in part because of how ruthless he was. While I was with him he was exceedingly forthcoming, but afterward, he called me out of the blue and said, "I just want to let you know, if you screw me on this story, I'll squash you like a squirrel in the road."

A few summers ago, when Tony Romo was dating Jessica Simpson, I spent an hour or so with Romo at training camp in California. He talked about his days at home in the off-season throwing the football into couch cushions. Spiral after spiral after spiral. At the time, the tag on Romo was that he was a celebrity first and a quarterback second. But I thought, *I'd like to reserve my judgment on this guy. I think he likes to play football very, very much. He's interesting. . . .*

Always interesting, the Cowboys. And perhaps more than any single franchise in the league, they've helped to make the NFL *big*—big like Jerry Jones's new stadium in Arlington. Maybe at times the Cowboys are a little too much Paris Hilton and not enough Paul Brown. Maybe they are America's Team to many, and America's team to root against for many more. But for the last half century, the Dallas Cowboys have been the most charismatic, compelling and magnetic team in football. ★

★ SUPER BOWL XII: *Cowboys 27, Broncos 10* ★

★ SUPER BOWL VI: *Cowboys 24, Dolphins 3* ★

Dallas
Cow

Sports Illustrated

boys

★ *Beneath the hole in the roof of Texas Stadium, the Cowboys' home for 38 seasons, Troy Aikman guided the Dallas attack in '94 against Arizona.*

The ★ 19

★ HOWLEY ★　　★ NILAND ★　　★ MEREDITH ★　　★ HAYES ★　　★ PERKINS ★

The decade began with a winless season but

60ˢ

★ JORDAN ★   ★ LILLY ★   ★ RENTZEL ★   ★ ANDRIE ★   ★ GREEN ★

ended with a winner on the brink of a title

★ *Already a master of the stoic look in '62, Tom Landry molded his collection of raw rookies and league leftovers into an NFL power in just seven seasons.*

1960

BORN IN AN NFL STORM

AMIDST NASTY LEAGUE POLITICS, THE DALLAS FRANCHISE FOUND A POWERFUL ALLY

BY TEX MAULE

Excerpted from
SPORTS ILLUSTRATED
February 8, 1960

THE CONTENTIOUS OWNERS OF the National Football League spent a long, acrimonious week in Miami Beach selecting a new commissioner to replace Bert Bell and deciding that it would be wise to admit Dallas to their select circle as a 13th franchise. On the surface, disturbed as it was, the issues seemed clear-cut. Beneath the surface there were complex undercurrents of tension and personal antipathy. The owners were not just fighting for the fun of it, as some facile reports from Miami Beach implied. They were fighting for serious stakes, and some of their maneuverings would have done credit to backroom pros at a political convention. ★ The accomplishments at this marathon meeting were simple: 1) Alvin Ray (Pete) Rozelle, a charming, able man of 33 who had been signally successful as general manager of the once besieged

★ *The brass—(clockwise from upper left) Murchison Jr., Wynne Jr., Landry and Schramm—got good news.*

Los Angeles Rams franchise, was elected commissioner; 2) Dallas did come into the league (to begin play in 1960), and Minneapolis–St. Paul was admitted for a year later.

The architect of expansion was George Halas, the founder, owner and coach of the Chicago Bears. Halas is ordinarily a quiet man, calm and serious behind thick, horn-rimmed glasses. The mildness can be deceptive; you have to watch him ranting on the sidelines at a football game to understand the violence and determination which underlie his being. He has been a part of professional football since its inception, and he has a real dedication to it—and to his personal creation, the Chicago Bears.

When the new American Football League was formed in August of 1959, Halas became convinced that the NFL had to fight back with strength against the budding competition. As longtime chairman of the NFL expansion committee, Halas had already explored the possibilities of granting franchises to several cities, among them Dallas and Minneapolis–St. Paul. At Bert Bell's funeral he conducted a quick, informal poll of the NFL owners, and after these soundings took it upon himself to commit the NFL irrevocably to expansion to those two cities.

But aside from this, Halas had an even more compelling personal reason for enlarging the league. Chicago is the only two-team city in the NFL. Halas is forced to share this rich market with the Chicago Cardinals, owned by Mr. and Mrs. Walter Wolfner. He has offered the Wolfners as much as $500,000 to move their franchise elsewhere, but Violet Wolfner is a stubborn woman who considers that the Cardinals have as much right to be in Chicago as the Bears do. Besides this—or because of it—she has a strong dislike for Halas.

Aside from competition at the gate, which is negligible, Halas would like to get the Cardinals out of Chicago so that he can cut a bigger share of the television cake. All of the other clubs in the NFL televise their road games back to their home cities, realizing a nice profit from the deal. Halas cannot do this because when the Bears are on the road the Cardinals are at home, and league rules forbid televising a game into a league city where the home team is playing. What's more, Halas is fully aware of the fact that the Cardinals depend heavily upon an extensive TV market in the South for their profits, and a Texas team would cut into the Cardinal TV market in Texas. Halas knew that if the Cardinals TV income was diminished, the

Wolfners would very likely be unable to stay in Chicago. What he was unable to accomplish by offering money, he set out to do more deviously.

HILE HALAS WAS fighting his undercover war for expansion, the rest of the owners were haggling with each other over the selection of a commissioner. The old guard of the league favored Austin Gunsel, who was pro tem commissioner after the death of Bell. They wanted the league office to stay in Philadelphia, where it had always been, and they wanted a commissioner who was amenable to suggestion. Solidly aligned against them was a bloc of seven teams voting for Marshall Leahy, the attorney for the San Francisco 49ers. Leahy, a freckled, husky man with

★ *Halas, boss of the Bears, had his own reasons for wanting Dallas in the league and played the political game perfectly.*

a forceful personality, suited the seven teams' needs perfectly. He was every bit as strong as Bell had been, but he was oriented more toward the new teams in the league than toward the old.

In the bitter fight which raged for nearly a full week and for 23 ballots, Halas never voted. He sat quietly in the meetings, passing when the vote came to him. Halas felt reasonably sure of nine of the 10 votes he needed to ensure expansion; he cared very little about whom would be elected commissioner and refrained from joining the long drawn-out arguments. He did not want to offend any of his supporters and he took no sides.

The schism between the two groups ran deep. "It's

 THE NEWS OF the admission of Dallas to the NFL was received joyfully by the Cowboys' owners, who had been waiting all week. They'd nearly given up hope.

the last stand of the old power elite of this league," one owner said, "the men who dominated pro football for 20 years. Their time has passed now. They don't own the biggest parks or best teams, and they can't wield the power they used to. You remember the old picture, *Stag at Bay*? These are stags at bay. And they haven't a chance against the wolves."

The logjam was finally broken by Wellington Mara of the New York Giants and Paul Brown of the Cleveland Browns. They settled upon Rozelle as a compromise candidate, and the tall, persuasive young man was elected on the first ballot on which his name appeared. Immediately after Rozelle's election, Halas's shrewd refusal to take part in the bitter fight over a commissioner paid off. His expansion program passed when Mara joined Halas's nine sure votes, giving him the 10 needed to put over expansion and admit Dallas in 1960 as the 13th team, playing against each club in both divisions.

News of the admission of Dallas to the NFL was received joyfully by the Dallas NFL owners, who had been waiting all week in the lobby of the Kenilworth. Bedford Wynne Jr. and Clint Murchison Jr., two immensely rich young Texas oilmen, and their general manager, Tex Schramm, had grown progressively gloomy through the long week of haggling over the commissioner. They had nearly given up hope of being admitted to the league in 1960.

Back in Dallas, where the owners of the new American Football League were meeting and voting Oakland in as their eighth franchise, the news that had proved so agreeable to Murchison, Wynne and Schramm was received with a great deal less enthusiasm. The reaction of the AFL owners, in fact, was quick and angry. Said commissioner Joe Foss, "This is an act of war. We will go to court or to Congress to prevent the NFL from putting the AFL franchise in Dallas [the Dallas Texans] out of business. You have antitrust laws to take care of such situations."

Here is where Pete Rozelle stepped in, giving promise that behind that deceptively ingratiating manner of his is a strong will. His reply to Foss was simple but direct: "They moved into our territory in New York and in Los Angeles and in San Francisco. Why shouldn't we be allowed to move into Dallas?"

Lamar Hunt, the young, serious and well-heeled Texan who owns the AFL Dallas franchise and who founded the league itself, had an answer to that: "It's not the same at all. In our case it's just like a little dog going into the big backyard of a big dog. But in their case it's the big dog going into the little backyard and asking the little bitty dog if there's not room for him. It's the size of the backyard that counts." ★

POSTSCRIPT *The Dallas Cowboys played their first regular season NFL game on Sept. 24, 1960 in the Cotton Bowl, losing to the Pittsburgh Steelers, 35–28, before an estimated crowd of 30,000 (though some reports had the figure as low as 13,000). They finished their first season 0-11-1, the high point being a 31–31 tie with the New York Giants. For three years the Cowboys dueled with Lamar Hunt's Dallas Texans for the affections of local football fans. Also playing in the Cotton Bowl, the Texans touted homegrown talent such as Cotton Davidson (Baylor), Jack Spikes (TCU) and Abner Haynes (North Texas State), and won the AFL Championship in their third season. But in 1963 Hunt, discouraged by poor attendance and the ongoing civic battle with the Cowboys, moved his team to Kansas City where it became the Chiefs.*

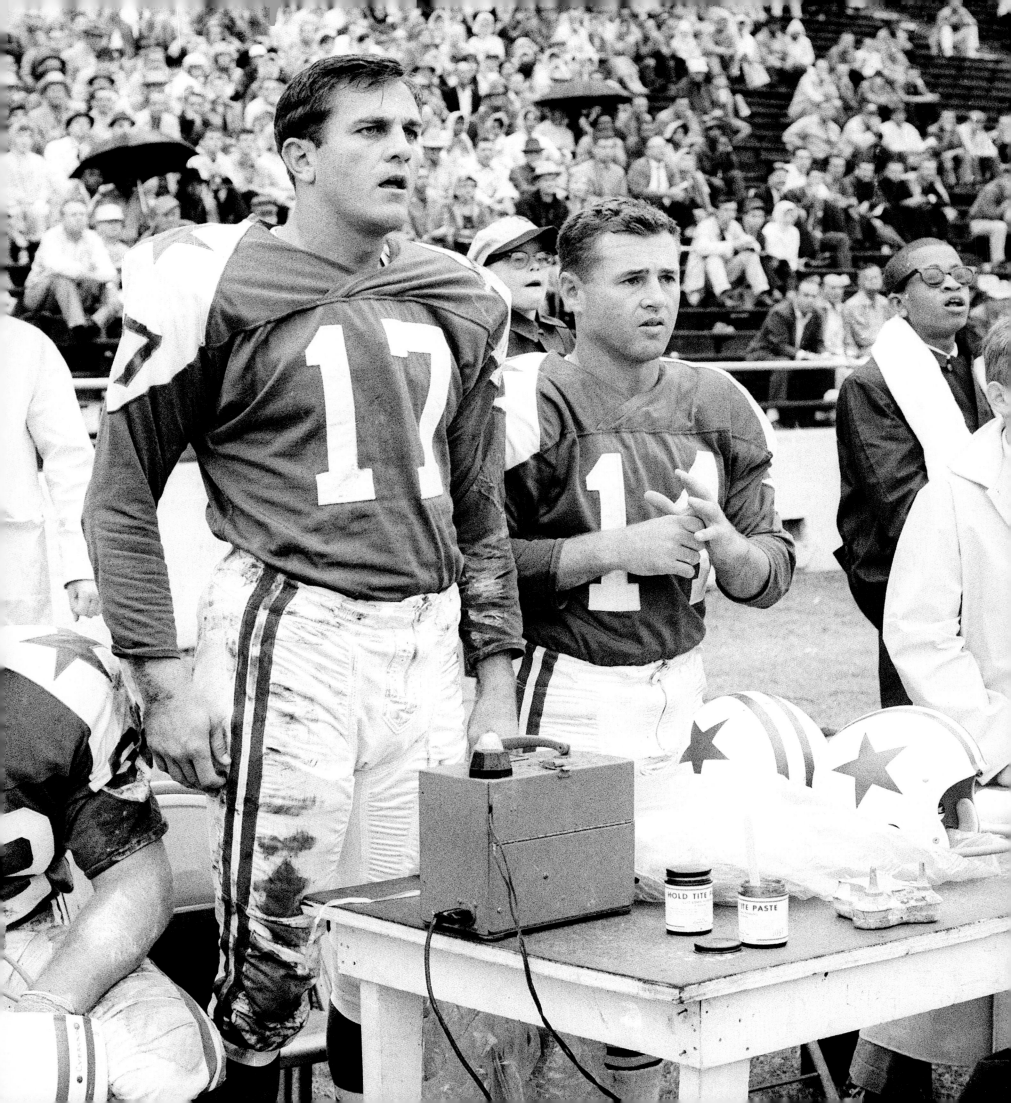

1962

WINNING WITH THE LANDRY PLAN

THE YOUNG COWBOYS PROSPERED WITH TWO QBS—AND A ROSTER FULL OF REJECTS

BY TEX MAULE

HE EXTRAORDINARY DALLAS Cowboys, playing only their third season in the National Football League and depending largely on other teams' rejects, free agents and a few draft choices, have suddenly developed into a potent NFL power. This achievement by a team that two years ago managed to win only one game points up two amazing accomplishments by the Cowboys management: first, a radical departure from football custom, discovered quite accidentally by young coach Tom Landry, a super organization man who normally doesn't believe in accidents; and, second, a scouting system that finds and utilizes talents in players others have long since given up on. ★ What Landry discovered was that if he alternated his quarterbacks on every play he was not only using the best offensive brain available—his—but he was also giving his quarterbacks,

Excerpted from
SPORTS ILLUSTRATED
November 5, 1962

★ *The lanky Meredith and the diminutive LeBaron made an odd couple but an effective quarterback duo.*

Eddie LeBaron and Don Meredith, some very subtle and unexpected tactical advantages. This shuttle has worked so well that the NFL's highest-scoring offense now belongs to the Cowboys.

Tom Landry's new system came about simply because the poverty-stricken Cowboys did not have enough depth at any other position to risk using a second-stringer as a messenger boy. "We didn't have two of anything but quarterbacks," Landry says, "so we had to alternate LeBaron and Meredith. If we had had an extra guard or end, I probably would have used the same system as Paul Brown. But all we could spare was an extra quarterback."

To his own surprise, he found that what was a practical necessity had led him to a much more useful way to send information into a game. The principal defect in sending in every offensive play via a guard or tackle is that the recipient of the play—the quarterback—has no time to consider it, nor does he have any way to relay whatever tidbits of information he has picked up on the field of play back to the resident genius on the sideline.

Landry's system of messenger quarterbacks remedies both defects: The quarterback coming off the field can tell Landry the nuances of what he has discovered in action and the quarterback trotting from the sideline to the huddle to call the new play has time to reflect on it. This moment of introspection, according to both Meredith and LeBaron, is invaluable.

"I don't think we will always use this system," says Meredith, who is an ardent admirer of both Landry and LeBaron and a semiardent admirer of the shuttle. "But it works now and it has been a big help to me. Landry is a living IBM machine. He knows every defense in this league cold and he never forgets anything. The time I spend on the sideline with him is great experience."

Meredith, a young man whose insouciance has sometimes been mistaken for carelessness, appreciates the value of these briefing sessions on the sideline. "You learn to analyze plays more quickly," he says. "I think it helps me with the big problem a quarterback has—gaining confidence. Tom always explains to us exactly why he is calling a play, and he's never wrong. He is a fantastic man. Most people don't know exactly what they want, but Tom does—in every facet of this game."

LeBaron, almost as much as Landry, has contributed to the education of Meredith as a pro quarterback.

Eddie is a small man—5' 7" and 168 pounds—but very strong. He has never, in his 10-year pro career, missed a game because of injuries. He rooms with Meredith, and LeBaron has been unsparing in his efforts to make Don a topflight pro.

"When I came up to the Redskins, Sammy Baugh was the quarterback," LeBaron says. "He helped me. He built my confidence whenever I got discouraged. Don doesn't need much help. He's going to be a fine quarterback."

It is not necessary for LeBaron to spend much time building Meredith's confidence, for Meredith is a self-confident man. As such, he is not wholly comfortable in the shuttle system. "I recognize its value," he says. "But a quarterback who is in all the way gets the feel of the game. That's why I say I don't think we'll use this system all the time from now on."

"TOM LANDRY is a living IBM machine," says Meredith, an ardent admirer. "He knows every defense in this league cold and he never forgets anything."

Part of the reason for this consistency is the fact that Landry, as a sideline quarterback, is not a pattern signal-caller. "He can pick apart defenses better than anyone I have ever seen," LeBaron says. "But he doesn't build from play to play, because that establishes a pattern the defense can begin to count on. He calls each play as a separate thing. This destroys the other team's ability to count on frequencies."

"Frequencies" is one of those words that show how pro football has advanced into its own computer era. "Most teams in this league chart your games and discover your frequency pattern: how often, from a certain formation, you call a certain play," explains Landry. "For instance, with third down and short yardage, with a halfback flanked and an end spread, you may run off tackle eight out of 10 times. If you line up like that, the defensive players automatically think, "Off tackle." So

we often shift into a different offensive formation just before the snap of the ball. There is a lag between the time the opposing players recognize the new formation and can recall what their frequency chart tells them. All of them can't react immediately. What I am trying to do is create that moment of hesitancy."

Landry not only is a fine tactician, he is a good judge of football talent and a precise organizer. Unlike most teams in professional football, the Cowboys have depended for much of their talent on free agents and late draft choices. Gil Brandt, the Cowboy talent scout, spends some six months of the year touring the nation looking at college football players. In his small room in the Cowboy offices in Dallas he has three tall filing cases filled with 255 big loose-leaf notebooks

While LeBaron was on the field, Meredith got the benefit of the brainy Landry on the sideline before shuttling in for his turn.

detailing the strengths and weaknesses of more than 3,000 college football players. From this vast array of information come the clues that have allowed the Cowboys to pick up players like Amos Marsh, their fullback, as free agents. Marsh is ninth in the league in rushing and is getting better each Sunday.

"We didn't have a draft our first year in the league," Landry says. "That was a terrible handicap, but it did one good thing. We had to pick players who had just one pro quality. Then we had to have the patience to develop the rest of the qualities a good pro needs. Marsh, for instance, had speed. No one drafted him, but he could run the 100 in 9.5 and we needed speed, so we signed him. We put him at fullback and waited. Now he's fine."

Mike Dowdle, picked up on waivers, has become one of the most promising linebackers in the business, even though he was a running back at Texas. Injuries forced the Cowboys to use him at linebacker. Chuck Howley, the other corner linebacker, was picked up by the Cowboys after being cut by the Chicago Bears.

One of the Cowboys' rookie defensive backs is Cornell Green, brother of Pumpsie Green, the second baseman for the Red Sox. Green had never played college football, although he was all-state in high school in Richmond, Calif. He approached Gil Brandt at a Utah State football game (Green was an All-America basketball player at Utah State) and asked for a chance. Probably no other team in pro football would have tried him. The Cowboys did, and although he is not first-string now, he certainly will be in a couple of years.

Before the Cardinals game last week, Meredith, chewing on a long, thin cigar, looked into the future. "I may or may not be the quarterback," he said, "but in the next couple of years, maybe sooner, the Cowboys are going to be right at the top year after year. Landry knows just what kind of personnel he wants at each position, and he knows precisely what he wants to do with them. He's pretty close right now to what he wants. When he gets it, the Cowboys and the Packers will be playing for the championship." ★

POSTSCRIPT *The Landry shuttle would not last long. The following season, Meredith established himself as the starting quarterback. He would not lead the Cowboys to a winning season until 1966, when they finished 10-3-1; but, true to Meredith's prophecy, they played in the NFL Championship Game that season against the Green Bay Packers. Though Dallas lost that game, 34–27, the young franchise had joined the NFL elite.*

1968

SO COLD, AND SO CLOSE

IN BITTER CONDITIONS, DALLAS COULD TASTE A FIRST TITLE UNTIL IT WAS SNATCHED AWAY BY THE PACKERS

BY TEX MAULE

IN THE GELID CONFINES of Lambeau Field, on the coldest New Year's Eve in the cold history of Green Bay, the Green Bay Packers shook off more than two quarters of almost total ineffectiveness and in the final frozen moments toiled 68 yards in four minutes and 37 seconds to score on the brave Dallas Cowboys defenders. With only 13 seconds left to play, Green Bay went ahead 21–17 to take the National Football League championship for the third straight year. Fuzzy Thurston, who has been around for six Green Bay titles, wiped tears from his eyes and beamed with a bright red, frozen face. "This," he said, "was the hardest one of my six. And the best."

The Packers had secured a 14–0 lead in the second quarter, but Dallas defensive end Willie Townes then hit Packers quarterback Bart Starr and forced a fumble; George Andrie picked up the ball and scored. A field goal by Danny Villanueva made it 14–10 at the half. On the first play of the fourth quarter, from midfield, Cowboys halfback Dan Reeves hit Lance Rentzel with a dramatic touchdown pass to take a 17–14 lead. With 4:50 left in the game, the Packers took possession at their 31-yard line and drove to the Dallas one. It was first-and-goal with 54 seconds left in the game.

From the one Starr twice called on running back Donny Anderson, and both times Anderson was stopped for no gain. After each play, Starr called for timeout. The second time he trotted over to confer with head coach Vince Lombardi. This was Green Bay's last timeout. There were 20 seconds and possibly two downs remaining. A field goal was a near certainty and would have put the game into a sudden-death overtime; a pass would win if completed; it would stop the clock and leave time for another play if not. Lombardi, who has unbounded faith in Starr, elected to gamble with his quarterback. "I was thinking of the fans," he said later, facetiously. "I couldn't stand to think of them sitting in those cold stands for an overtime period."

Anderson had slipped taking off on both of his jabs at the line. The field, now in the shadow of the stands, was an iced-over pond. "I knew Donny wasn't getting any footing," Starr said after the game. "I figured I wouldn't have as far to run and I wouldn't have as much chance to fumble, so I called the wedge to Kramer's side." Right guard Jerry Kramer had been having much better luck blocking Jethro Pugh than guard Gale Gillingham had had with Bob Lilly.

"When he called the play, I knew he would be following me," Kramer explained. "I had been having a hell of a time trying to drive off and block. I searched around with both feet and I finally found a little soft spot with my right foot. I got off real good with the ball. Pugh was playing on my inside shoulder—to my left—and I took my best shot at him. That may have been the biggest block I ever made in my life."

The block moved Pugh in and back. Starr came hard behind him and slid into the end zone, and suddenly, for 50,000 people, spring came. ★

POSTSCRIPT *The game, perhaps the most famous loss in Cowboys' history, would ever after be known as the Ice Bowl. The windchill factor was measured at –46°. At halftime Don Meredith, who was diagnosed with pneumonia after the game, had cut a hole in his jersey so he could warm his passing hand against his belly. Two weeks later, the Packers would beat the Oakland Raiders 33–14 in what would officially become known as Super Bowl II. It was played in Miami, where the temperature was 100° warmer than for the game in Green Bay.*

★ *On the fateful play, Starr (15) slithered into the end zone for the winning score, leaving the gallant Cowboys frozen out.*

Excerpted from SPORTS ILLUSTRATED *January 8, 1968*

THE 1960s TEXAS STYLE

COW BELLES

1st Row — left to right: Sally Singleton, Jeannette Gaddis, Nelda Tate, Patty Saunders, Carolyn Duggan. 2nd Row — left to right: Mary McCord, Sandy Hill, Phyllis Angona, Mary Glen Joy, Jeanenne Grammer, Vickie Billion, Barbara Eason.

★ Before his notoriety for killing Lee Harvey Oswald in 1963, Jack Ruby operated a popular Dallas strip joint, called the Carousel Club.

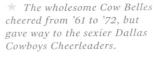

★ The wholesome Cow Belles cheered from '61 to '72, but gave way to the sexier Dallas Cowboys Cheerleaders.

★ Texas-born Dr Pepper was the locals' favorite "soft drink" (never "soda pop" in these parts), to be enjoyed three times a day, as the logo indicated.

★ 7-Eleven originated in Dallas in 1927, sprouted stores all over Texas in the '40s and '50s, and became the Southland Corp. in '61.

WARREN BEATTY
FAYE DUNAWAY

THEY'RE YOUNG...
THEY'RE IN LOVE...
AND THEY
KILL PEOPLE

BONNIE AND CLYDE.

MICHAEL J. POLLARD · GENE HACKMAN · ESTELLE PARSONS
DAVID NEWMAN and ROBERT BENTON Charles Strouse WARREN BEATTY ARTHUR PENN TECHNICOLOR® FROM WARNER BROS.-SEVEN ARTS RELEASED THROUGH WARNER-PATHE

★ Clyde Barrow and Bonnie Parker, both born near Dallas, robbed banks in Technicolor in the Oscar-winning 1967 film.

★ Lyndon B. Johnson, the dominant Texas politician of the decade, gave the cowboy new status.

★ Big Tex, with a booming voice welcoming one and all each October to "The Great State Fair of Texas," sported the Lee brand of Western wear in the '60s.

Dr Pepper ("The Friendly Pepper-Upper") became a '60s sponsor of *Dick Clark's American Bandstand* show on TV.

THE 1960s IN PICTURES

★ *"Bullet Bob" Hayes (22) and "Dandy Don" Meredith (17) made a dangerous duo in '68, combining for eight touchdown passes in a 12–2 season.*
★ *Hayes, once a star sprinter at Florida A&M, is the only man to win both an Olympic gold medal (100m, 4×100m) and a Super Bowl ring.*

★ LB Mike Dowdle (30) and DT Guy Reese pinned the Giants'
    Joe Morrison in a '62 loss, but were en route to a best-yet five wins.

(FROM LEFT) JAMES DRAKE; WALTER IOOSS JR.

★ Defensive hero Bob Lilly chased Y.A. Tittle of the Giants before
    29,653 in the Cotton Bowl, second largest home crowd of '63.

★ In a '66 game, DE George Andrie, Pro Bowler and defensive fixture of early Cowboys teams, sacked Redskins QB Sonny Jurgensen.
★ Savvy running back Dan Reeves (later head coach of the Broncos), sailed over longtime Dallas lineman Ralph Neely (73) in '66.

★ *Eddie LeBaron, all 5' 7", 168 pounds of him, was dubbed the "Littlest General" and started at quarterback for the Cowboys' first three seasons.*

★ Calvin Hill's fine rookie season ended in the Cotton Bowl
muck as Cleveland won the '69 Eastern Conference title.

★ RB Don Perkins, here against the Redskins in '67, was one
of the first Cowboys stars; he joined the Ring of Honor in '76.

1960s: The Roundup

★ ALL-DECADE TEAM ★

OFFENSE

QB ★ DON MEREDITH (1960–68)

RB ★ DON PERKINS (1961–68)

FB ★ WALT GARRISON (1966–74)

WR ★ BOB HAYES (1964–74)

WR ★ FRANK CLARKE (1960–67)

TE ★ PETTIS NORMAN (1962–70)

T ★ BOB FRY (1960–64)

G ★ TONY LISCIO (1963–64, '66–71)

C ★ DAVE MANDERS (1964–66, '68–74)

G ★ JOHN NILAND (1966–74)

T ★ RALPH NEELY (1965–77)

K ★ DANNY VILLANUEVA (1965–67)

RET ★ BOB HAYES (1964–74)

DEFENSE

DE ★ LARRY STEPHENS (1963–67)

DT ★ BOB LILLY (1961–74)

DT ★ JETHRO PUGH (1965–78)

DE ★ GEORGE ANDRIE (1962–72)

LB ★ CHUCK HOWLEY (1961–73)

LB ★ LEE ROY JORDAN (1963–76)

LB ★ JERRY TUBBS (1960–67)

DB ★ MEL RENFRO (1964–77)

DB ★ CORNELL GREEN (1962–74)

DB ★ DON BISHOP (1960–65)

DB ★ MIKE GAECHTER (1962–69)

P ★ RON WIDBY (1968–71)

COACH ★ TOM LANDRY (1960–88)

BEST DRAFT SURPRISE

ROGER STAUBACH QB NAVY ▶
1964 Drafted 10th round, 129th overall

Tex Schramm selected the 1963 Heisman Trophy winner a year before most teams believed him to be available, knowing that Staubach's one year at New Mexico Military Institute before Navy accelerated his eligibility. Schramm was undaunted by the fact that Staubach had to fullfill a four-year tour of duty in the Navy.

BIGGEST DRAFT BUST

DENNIS HOMAN WR ALABAMA 1968
Drafted 1st round, 20th overall

The Cowboys picked the Crimson Tide All-America in hopes of starting him alongside Bob Hayes. In three seasons in Dallas, Homan caught just 23 passes. The Cowboys wouldn't draft another receiver in Round I for nearly two decades when they took Mike Sherrard of UCLA with the 18th overall pick in 1986.

★ A COWBOY TO REMEMBER *With a 29-year tenure—as long as Tom Landry's—LB Jerry Tubbs, No. 50, went from expansion draftee to leading tackler to linebackers coach.*

Steady, Eddie: At the Cowboys' first training camp in 1960, QB LeBaron saddled DT Ed Husmann—perhaps the team's first photo op.

> BY THE NUMBERS

.269 Tom Landry's career winning percentage when he was given the ultimate vote of confidence by Tex Schramm and owner Clint Murchison, a 10-year contract extension in February 1964.

.646 Landry's winning percentage over the next 24 seasons.

196 Consecutive regular-season games played by Bob Lilly beginning on Sept. 17, 1961 and lasting the full length of his Cowboys career, through his final game on Dec. 14, 1974.

21,417 Average attendance at the Cotton Bowl for Cowboys games during 1960, the franchise's inaugural season.

24,500 Average attendance at the Cotton Bowl for Dallas Texans games during 1960, the AFL franchise's inaugural season.

JIM BOEKE, OCTOBER 1966
Recalling when he was first signed by the Cowboys, as an offensive tackle and a 19th round draft pick:

" **I wasn't exactly a bonus baby. I went to coffee with the scout and when he offered me $6,500 I not only signed, I paid for the coffee.**

OVERLOOKED GAME OF THE DECADE

SEPTEMBER 17, 1961 VS. STEELERS After going winless in 1960, the Cowboys began their sophomore season in style, scoring 10 unanswered points in the final 56 seconds of the season opener in Dallas, for a 27–24 win. QB Eddie LeBaron threw for two long scores, to Frank Clarke (44 yards) and Billy Howton (45 yards), but it was his quarterback shuttle mate, Don Meredith, who tied the game with a 17-yard TD toss to Dick Bielski. Kicker Allen Green then sealed the team's first-ever victory with a game-winning 27-yard field goal.

WHAT WERE THEY THINKING?

IN THE SPRING OF 1967, unsatisfied with Danny Villanueva as their place-kicker, the Cowboys brass created a "Kicking Karavan," an open tryout tour that visited 29 cities across the country. Roughly 1,400 wanna-bees tried out on the Karavan, but the only kicker signed was Harold Deters, whom the Cowboys had actually drafted in the 12th round earlier that year. In three games as a Cowboy, Deters made just one of four field goal attempts and was promptly replaced—by Villanueva, who made 8 of 19 field goal tries in what was his final season.

★ IT'S A FACT: *The new Dallas NFL franchise changed its original name from Rangers to Cowboys, fearing conflict with the city's minor league baseball team.*

The ★ 19

It was an era of remarkable success as the

70s

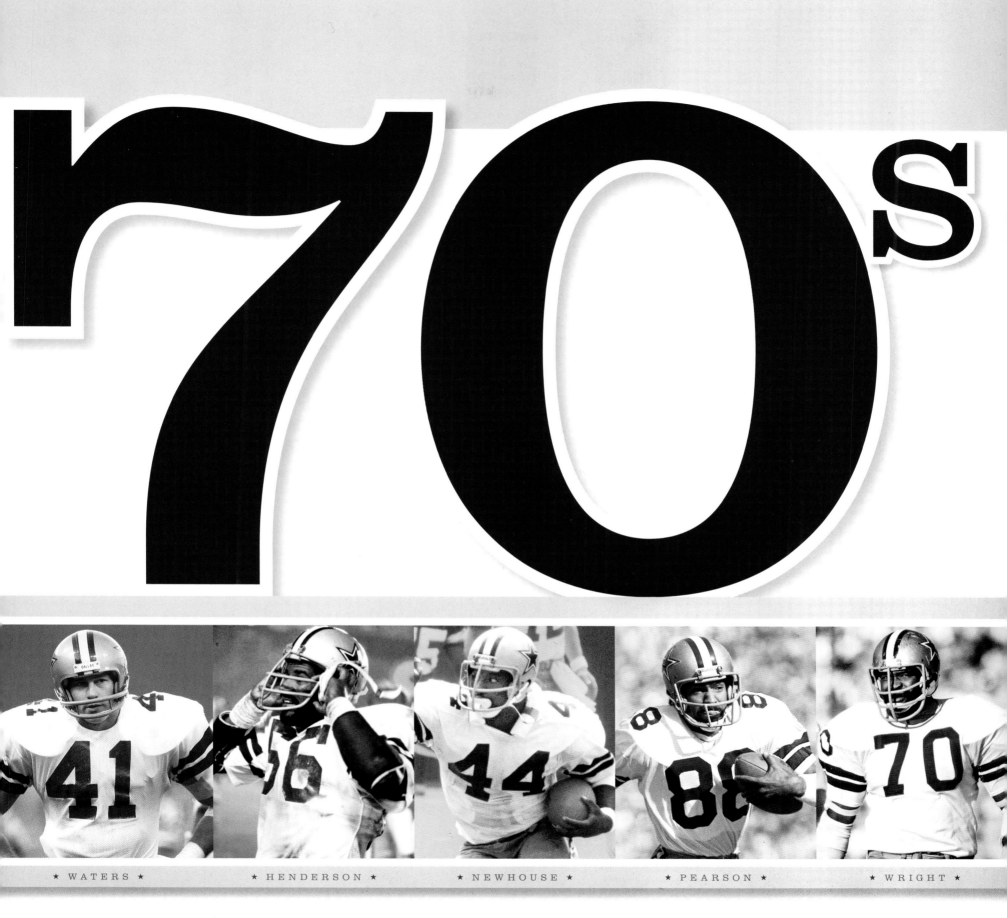

★ WATERS ★   ★ HENDERSON ★   ★ NEWHOUSE ★   ★ PEARSON ★   ★ WRIGHT ★

Cowboys went to five Super Bowls and won two

★ *Calvin Hill, a first-round draft pick in '69, struggled free against the Rams in '73 after a helmet-popping effort from All-Pro guard John Niland, a No. 1 pick in '66.*

1972

JUST LIKE THEY PLANNED IT

WITH TYPICAL SAVVY, DALLAS DOMINATED MIAMI FOR THEIR FIRST SUPER BOWL WIN

BY TEX MAULE

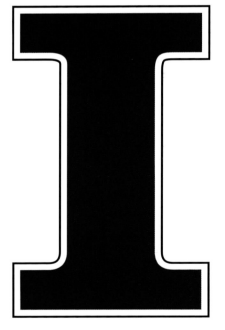

IT CAN TAKE A SPELL TO GET ALL THE BUGS out of a computer, but head programmer Tom Landry has finally got his Dallas Cowboys printing out to perfection. At least there wasn't any evidence of a breakdown on Sunday in New Orleans, where the Cowboys demolished the Miami Dolphins 24–3 on the Poly-Turf in Tulane Stadium in Super Bowl VI. In the process, they were all but unstoppable on the ground, with celebrated nonstop nontalker Duane Thomas, Walt Garrison and Calvin Hill amassing most of a Super Bowl–record 252 yards rushing and, once Roger Staubach got his receivers sorted out, overwhelming through the air as well. ★ Miami made three mistakes, all to its enduring sorrow. In the first period Larry Csonka, the burly running back who had not fumbled all season, lost touch with the ball on the Dallas 46, and linebacker Chuck Howley recovered for the Cowboys. Twelve plays later Mike Clark kicked a nine-yard field goal

Excerpted from
SPORTS ILLUSTRATED
January 24, 1972

★ *Hill was one of several Cowboys who together took off for a then record 252 rushing yards.*

that gave Dallas a lead it never relinquished. The Cowboys got their first touchdown on a seven-yard Staubach–to–Lance Alworth pass completing a 76-yard second-period drive. Miami's Garo Yepremian kicked a 31-yard field goal to make the score 10–3 and there still was the appearance of a contest as late as halftime. But not for long. The Cowboys wrapped it all up early in the third quarter, driving 71 yards in eight plays, Thomas going in from three yards out.

In truth the outcome had been signed, sealed and delivered long before—in point of fact, before the opening kickoff. So well had Landry—and the computers he uses to analyze opposing offenses and defenses—dissected the Dolphins in the days leading up to the Super Bowl that in only one small respect did he have to adjust his game plan. The Miami linebackers covered the Dallas running backs man for man on first-down passes, so Landry, who picks the plays for Staubach, reverted to his more usual practice of calling runs on that down.

Going into the game the Cowboys had expected to run up the middle, throw to their backs and seal off the most sharklike Dolphin, middle linebacker Nick Buoniconti. They did all of those things just about as the computer and Landry had predicted they could.

THE COWBOYS PREPARED themselves for this game with the precision that is their mark. The Dolphins, in their first Super Bowl, were being true to their nature too. Someone asked head coach Don Shula if his club was relaxed, and Shula, who has matured socially as well as professionally during his two years in Miami, smiled. "They are individuals," he said. "The ones who are always relaxed before a game are relaxed and the ones who are always tense and serious are tense and serious. I think it is a mistake to ask a club to be either one way or the other. What you want the players to do is be themselves and I think our players have been themselves this week."

"The Dolphins are a well-coached young football team," Dallas player-coach Dan Reeves said before the game. "That makes it fairly easy to prepare for them. Because they are disciplined and well-coached, you know exactly what they are going to do. They are not going to come up and play a defense you haven't seen. For an inexperienced club like Miami, the only way to play good football is to do the same thing over

and over again. You can't give them more offense or defense than they can handle."

However, Miami did present one thorny problem in the person of Buoniconti, who, though comparatively small for his position, is inordinately quick and intelligent. So the Dallas strategists concentrated on neutralizing him. The blocking the Cowboys planned to use to clear the way to Buoniconti was called doodad blocking by Vince Lombardi, who used it on power sweeps or cutbacks. In the modern, more sophisticated nomenclature of the Cowboys, it is referred to as slip-wedge blocking.

Center Dave Manders and All-Pro guard John Niland were given the responsibility for making the technique work. "We plan to run over the middle on them when they are in an odd line," Niland explained before the game. "Our backs are the key. They have to make a good fake to the right, to take Buoniconti a step or two in that direction, then cut back over the middle. Manders and I will contain the man playing over the center's head—wedge him—then one of us will slide off and take Buoniconti in the direction he has started to go. If we can seal off Buoniconti, then Thomas or Hill or Garrison should have running room."

 "LANDRY IS THE quietest guy in the world when he's losing, but if he beats you, he gigs you a little bit," said Reeves. And now Landry gigged the Dolphins.

If Buoniconti presented a special problem to Dallas, All-Pro tackle Bob Lilly presented just as much of a challenge to Miami. Ed Khayat, the coach of the Philadelphia Eagles, expatiated on that. "When you're getting ready to play Dallas, you spend about half your time trying to figure out how you're going to handle Lilly," he said. "And if you put as many men on him as you should, they have a lot of people who'll eat you alive."

In the Cowboys' third-quarter drive, Landry's meticulous preparation worked to perfection. The slip-wedge block sealed off Buoniconti, and Thomas sliced back off the right side for 23 yards to set up a first down on the Miami 22.

"Landry is the quietest guy in the world when he's losing, but if he beats you, he gigs you a little bit," Reeves had said, and now Landry, winning, gigged the Dolphins with a flanker reverse by Bob Hayes good for 16 yards and a first down at the Miami six. Thomas made his touchdown two plays later and the score was 17–3.

Early in the fourth period, the Cowboys' intimate knowledge of Miami's attack patterns again paid off. Miami had reached its own 49, with third-and-four coming up. Twice before, with third down and comparable yardage, quarterback Bob Griese had thrown to running back Jim Kiick, completing the pass both times. So, sure enough, Griese called the same play and the Dolphins made their second mistake of the game. Howley was lying in wait for the ball. He picked it off in front of the flabbergasted Kiick and ran 41 yards to the Miami nine. Howley wasn't tackled at the nine; he just stumbled and fell. "Please don't mention that," he said. "I'm embarrassed."

His pratfall made no real difference. From the nine, Staubach took the Cowboys to a touchdown in three plays. A seven-yard pass to tight end Mike Ditka made

the score 24–3 and the Miami fans, who have a tradition of waving white handkerchiefs every time their heroes score, used them to wipe away the tears.

Later, in the quiet, dispirited Dolphins dressing room, Griese was asked for perhaps the 40th time if he had felt frustrated during the game. He sighed and said, "A number of times, my man, a number of times."

"The way I see it," Staubach was saying at about the same time in the Dallas dressing room, "was that in today's game my people were doing a lot of things right and maybe Griese's were doing a lot of things wrong."

Which is what the manager of the Cowboys' computer company had once told Cowboys president Tex Schramm, only he put it more vividly. Speaking of the value of computers, he said, "You put garbage in, you get garbage out."

There is no garbage on the Dallas Cowboys. Not anymore. ★

POSTSCRIPT *The game marked the zenith and the end of the short and strange Cowboys career of Duane Thomas, who gained 95 rushing yards on the afternoon. On media day, he had refused to answer questions and sat silently; a week after the game, Staubach, who was named the game's MVP, suggested that the award would have gone to Thomas had he cooperated with the press. In the postgame locker room, CBS reporter Tom Brookshier asked Thomas a long, muddled question that, in essence, was, "Are you as fast as you seem?" To which Thomas famously replied, "Evidently."*

★ *With his meticulous game plan, Landry outstrategized Shula, Buoniconti and the Dolphins, earning himself a joyride.*

1973

TWO GOOD MEN, JUST ONE JOB

MAKING THE CALL: MORTON OR STAUBACH? IN DALLAS, THE QB QUANDARY PERSISTED

BY EDWIN SHRAKE

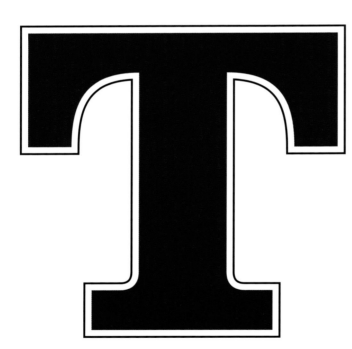

UGLY FAT.
You can't be fat . . . and fast, too. Fat is hard to see, fat is hard to detect. It hides under thick skin, it enslaves and slows every movement of the body . . . an untrained eye cannot find fat. LIFT. RUN. DIET. WORK. —T.L.

HE T.L. MEANS TOM LANDRY. Ralph Neely, the tackle, was lying on his back lifting weights with his feet. Looking between his knees, Neely could see the UGLY FAT sign on the wall of the Cowboys' practice field clubhouse in north Dallas. It was late on a Wednesday afternoon, and the Cowboys had been running plays for hours. Most of the linemen were heading toward the clubhouse now, their heads down and their breathing hard, but Roger Staubach and Craig Morton were still over by the goalposts throwing passes, as if the last one left on the field might be the first one in Tom Landry's heart come Sunday. Staubach and Morton have both been starting quarterbacks for Dallas in the Super Bowl, and neither believes he ought to be No. 2. To Neely it does not matter which one is in the game. ★ Few of the Cowboys are what you would call close

Excerpted from
SPORTS ILLUSTRATED
December 10, 1973

★ *The intense, ultracompetitive Staubach gained the upper hand on Morton in their starter's duel.*

pals but certainly they know each other well enough, and if there is any real disagreement over who ought to be the quarterback, it is hard to detect. Unless, of course, you ask Staubach or Morton.

"I used to care," Neely said, resting a moment. "I used to prefer having Craig in there. But now I can honestly say I think they're equal. Roger will sacrifice anything, even his own body, to win a game. Craig is more cool and calm."

Neely did another dozen lifts and sat up. "Craig has taken so much hell here that he can stay calm now even when they're booing him," he said. "Roger hasn't lived through anything like it. He doesn't really know what it's like when they get down on you. Don Meredith knew, and Craig found out in a hurry."

The two quarterbacks finally walked past the sweating Neely and into the clubhouse. "Look, I'm a lineman, so the quarterback can't give me anything," Neely said. "He can't throw me a pass or let me run with the ball, so there's no reason for me to play favorites. It just happens to be true that Craig and Roger are about the same on the field in terms of effectiveness," he continued. "They're not all that different off the field, either. Roger is supposed to be Mr. Pure, dedicated and all that, a sincere family man. Craig is supposed to be a playboy. Well, Craig got that image because he's a bachelor. But underneath, Craig is just as dedicated as Roger. Craig is the kind of guy who'll drive down to Waco and spend half the night with a sick child who wrote him a letter and then won't ever mention it."

Neely wiped his face and glanced up at the UGLY FAT sign. "You don't think T.L.'s trying to tell us something, do you?" he said.

Morton walked out of training camp this year after being offered a contract that was heavy with incentive clauses. He figured incentive clauses are not worth much to a man on the bench, and refused to sign. Staubach said in the off-season that he wanted to be No. 1 or be traded. "Being Number 2 around here is like being a rookie," he said. "They treat you as if you aren't even there. I don't have that many years for pro football." Dallas is not about to trade Roger Staubach. So if Landry and general manager Tex Schramm had to make any of their quarterbacks unhappy, it would not be him.

"I've never seen a player as uniquely popular as Staubach," Schramm said. "Staubach came along when the public was getting tired of hearing about guys like Joe Namath. Roger is the All-America hero type. He

"I HAVE NEVER seen a player as uniquely popular as Staubach," says Schramm. "He's the All-America hero type. He could do endless endorsements. He'll wind up rich."

could make more money than any football player in history. He could make a speech every night of the year at $1,500 a pop if he wanted to, and he could do endless commercials and endorsements in a way that has never happened to Morton. And he's cautious about investing his money. He'll wind up rich."

ROM THE OUTSIDE, WELlingtons looks like an adobe fort. It sits in a garden on a small lake across from a runway at Love Field in Dallas. The jets come over low enough that their engines whine through the din of discothèque music inside the building, which is usually crowded with young businessmen and pretty girls. Wellingtons has three bars, including one on the roof and another on a darkened second floor furnished with couches. "The second floor's for necking," said a downstairs bartender. "You never saw so many pretty ladies as come in this place," he said. In fact Wellingtons is often so crowded that Morton will not go inside, and until recently he was one of the three owners.

After declaring bankruptcy a few years ago and borrowing against his salary, Morton has pretty well pulled himself out of it now, partly by giving up big houses with swimming pools and partly because he decided to quit giving his money to anyone asking for it. "The hardest word I ever learned to say is 'no,'" Morton said one evening in Wellingtons while girls circled the table, hoping to draw his eye. Morton is big and good-looking, and even his being a semihero does not drive them off.

His style of living has never been half as wild as many people would like to suppose. Some of his attitudes are almost prim. "I'm a closed person," he said.

★ *Morton took a typical quarterback's beating on the field, but he also had to suffer the jeers of partisan Cowboys fans.*

"I don't have many friends. I like the company of just a few. But for a while there, I wasn't very careful. When you're in the spotlight and you're seen laughing it up, people imagine all sorts of things." Morton and Staubach have adjoining lockers at the practice clubhouse, at Texas Stadium and at most of the road games. Reporters gather around the one who has been more prominent, and the other can always hear what is said. "That can make for some awkward moments," Morton said, "but Roger and I both know the score. He's a compassionate guy." In October, Dallas lost three of four games. Staubach started all of them. "This has been the first time in a long time that everything wasn't right on the track for Roger," Morton said. "It's been a lot for him to go through. As for me, how'd you like the way I handled the ball on field goals and extra points?"

WILLPOWER
Intellect tires, the will never.
The brain needs sleep, the will none.
The whole body is nothing but objectified will.
The whole nervous system constitutes the
*   antennae of the will.*
Every action of the body is nothing but the
*   act of the will objectified....*   —T.L.

Roger Staubach has never been short on willpower. "I don't care if it's golf or pool or what, I love to win," he said. "You can carry that attitude too far, of course. But in pro football winning is all there is. If you don't win, you haven't done what the game is about. I meant it when I said I wouldn't want to stay here unless I was number 1. It's a human reaction to root against the guy you're trying to beat out. That's a bad position to be in, and it's bad for the team, but I don't see how you can help it." ★

POSTSCRIPT *Morton would be traded mid-season the next year to the New York Giants, and again three years later to the Denver Broncos. Staubach would never again relinquish the starter's job; from 1973 through the '79 season, when he retired, he would start every game but two for the Cowboys. On Jan. 15, 1978, the Cowboys met the Broncos in Super Bowl XII. It was Staubach versus Morton, a duel won by Staubach, 27–10. Staubach would later go on to become chairman and CEO of The Staubach Co., a multibillion dollar real estate operation. As Schramm had once predicted for the young quarterback, he wound up rich.*

1974

THE MAD BOMBER SAVED THE DAY

IN A THANKSGIVING GAME TO REMEMBER, ROOKIE BACKUP QB CLINT LONGLEY PERFORMED A MIRACLE

BY EDWIN SHRAKE

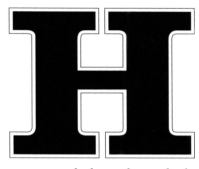

HERE IS CLINT Longley, 22 years old, bold and scattered-looking in a boyish way, the nice kid from the next ranch down the road who has a peculiar twist for catching rattlesnakes and blasting away at stumps and bushes with his two six-guns. Clint is standing on the sideline at Texas Stadium, noting on a clipboard the play that the third-place Dallas Cowboys have just run in the third quarter this Thanksgiving Day afternoon against the second-place Washington Redskins. All of a sudden he hears a voice: "Longley, get your helmet."

For a moment Longley can't find his helmet. He hadn't figured he would need it. He is a rookie quarterback who would have been playing for Abilene Christian College instead of Dallas this fall if he hadn't decided to go ahead and graduate last summer. Longley looks up and sees Roger Staubach, the No. 1 quarterback, ambling off the field with glass eyeballs and a stoned frown. Staubach has been knocked goofy by a Redskins linebacker; he can walk, but he doesn't know where he is. Someone says to Longley, "Get 'em, Bomber." He got the nickname Mad Bomber in training camp when he threw a pass that clanged off an upper rung of Tom Landry's coaching tower. He has never played in a regular-season game.

★ *After his game-winning strike to Pearson stunned the Redskins, Longley was duly hoisted by his amazed teammates.*

The Cowboys are all but out of the playoffs for the first time since 1966. All the Redskins need to do to clinch a playoff spot is to hold on to a 16–3 lead. The Mad Bomber comes in. Staubach slumps on the bench with a towel around his neck and a popper at his nose, wondering where everybody went. In the huddle, fullback Walt Garrison starts to repeat a play he has brought in from Landry. Halfway through this lengthy recitation, Longley says, "Save your breath, I know the play."

In less than nine minutes the Mad Bomber takes Dallas to two touchdowns, one of them a 35-yard pass to Billy Joe DuPree. The Cowboys are ahead, 17–16, as the fourth quarter begins. The stadium is rocking with emotion.

The Redskins bust in for another touchdown and a 23–17 lead. With 35 seconds left and the ball at midfield, Landry sends in a play that requires Drew Pearson to run a down-and-in 20 yards deep. In the huddle Pearson suggests he fake instead, move inside and try to split the two defensive backs and race for the end zone. "What have we got to lose?" says Longley.

The Mad Bomber pumps and throws—and there is Pearson at the four-yard line, reaching up to take the ball over his shoulder and going on in to score. On the sideline you can feel the stadium quake as the energy released by one huge, incredible cry rockets around the walls and soars through the hole in the roof. ★

POSTSCRIPT *Longley would serve as a backup for only one more season with the Cowboys. In training camp before the 1976 season, he threw a blindside punch at Staubach's head after the two had argued over a negative comment Longley made about Pearson. He was promptly traded to San Diego where after one season his NFL career came to an end. His lone magical day, however, remains one the richest moments in Cowboys history.*

Excerpted from SPORTS ILLUSTRATED *December 9, 1974*

HEINZ KLUETMEIER

1976

ON A WING AND A PRAYER

THE COWBOYS SNATCHED A PLAYOFF WIN FROM THE DISBELIEVING VIKINGS WITH A MIRACULOUS PASS

BY DAN JENKINS

USUALLY IT ONLY HAPPENS in those novels written for young readers. It is cold and gloomy and all hope seems to be gone, but the good guy who loves his wife and family and country has gone back to try one more long pass against the evil villains who throw bottles and garbage at football officials. The ball sails high and far, 50 yards into the frozen atmosphere, a silly object, it seems, straining to be seen against the feeble lights that glow through the gray Minnesota sky. Now the ball is coming to earth as the scoreboard flickers away the final seconds of the game. There are two men underneath the ball and suddenly one of them slips and falls, and the one who is supposed to catch it and complete the grandest of comebacks and upsets and fairy tales does exactly that. Roger Staubach has thrown a pass to Drew Pearson, and the Dallas Cowboys have used up a lifetime of good fortune in a single play to stun the Minnesota Vikings. And now in the first round of the playoffs, the score will be entered into legend as Dallas 17, Minnesota 14, after Staubach and Pearson have driven a dagger into the heart of every seed planter on the Minnesota plain.

The Vikings, who had been outplayed the whole way by these surprising Cowboys, had nevertheless forged ahead 14–10 in the fourth quarter as Fran Tarkenton had somehow brought his team back on an off day. For their part the Cowboys looked disheartened, finished. With 44 seconds remaining, the Cowboys were on their own 25. Staubach fired a 25-yarder to Pearson, who went into the air at the sideline, made the first-down catch and was floated out-of-bounds by Nate Wright.

When Pearson went back to the Dallas huddle he told Staubach, "I can beat Wright deep, but give me a chance to catch my breath." After an incompletion, Staubach said only a couple of words in the huddle: "Streak route." Pearson began the streak down the sideline to his right. Wright and Pearson were in a footrace now as the ball went into the air. The ball was slightly underthrown and was going to reach its mooring somewhere around the Minnesota five-yard line. Pearson noticed this, but Wright did not. As Pearson pulled up, Wright went in front of him, and only Pearson and Wright will ever know whether there was any pushing off. Wright either slipped, tripped or was pushed to the grass just as Pearson turned and got his hands on the ball at his belt, then stepped into the end zone to the accompaniment of the most enormous swell of silence in the history of gatherings of 46,425 wearers of the purple.

No one knew for a matter of seconds that it actually was a touchdown. Everybody saw something orange or red flutter to the ground and thought it was an official's flag—obviously an interference call against either Pearson or Wright.

Even Pearson saw it. "When I looked again, it was a real orange," he said. And what it mostly was, of course, was a real touchdown. ★

POSTSCRIPT *In the game's final seconds, the Minnesota fans, outraged that no penalty was called, began throwing debris, including a pint whiskey bottle that hit field judge Armen Terzian on the forehead and knocked him to the ground. Moments after the game Tarkenton learned that his father had suffered a fatal heart attack while watching the game on television at home in Georgia. At about the same time, in his postgame press conference Staubach, a staunch Catholic, described the game-winning pass this way: "I closed my eyes and said a Hail Mary." The press seized on the phrase and the "Hail Mary pass" would become a staple of the football vernacular.*

★ *On the key play, Wright (43) went down, Pearson caught the ball (right hip)—and an orange (center), not a flag, hit the ground.*

Excerpted from SPORTS ILLUSTRATED *January 5, 1976*

1978

WELL, THAT WAS FUN

LED BY A DOOMSDAY DEFENSIVE DUO, DALLAS CRUSHED THE BRONCOS AND MADE IT LOOK EASY

BY DAN JENKINS

SUPER BOWL XII

AS SUPER BOWLS GO, the one played indoors last Sunday in New Orleans was way up there for mosts— it had the most fumbles, the most hitting, the most noise, the most penalties, the most tricky plays and no doubt the most X's and O's stamped on a coach's forehead, as Dallas's Tom Landry nailed Denver's Red Miller to a blackboard and left him there. And when last seen, the Cowboys' two biggest heroes, Randy White and Harvey Martin, were still lecturing the state of Colorado on the mysteries of the flex defense. As a final gesture of victory, another Cowboy star, linebacker Tom Henderson, went prancing down the field as the last seconds flashed off and jumped up and stuffed a football over the crossbar. Maybe he thought it was Craig Morton's right arm.

The score was Dallas 27 and Denver 10, but it seemed that close only if you were sitting on the Denver side of the Superdome. It was a case of the Cowboys doing just about whatever they wished on offense, and so thoroughly confusing the Broncos with their Doomsday II defensive genius and manpower and quickness that the Broncos assistant coaches upstairs on the headphones must have sounded as though they were under a kamikaze attack as they screamed down to the field with their guesses and remedies for poor Craig and poor Red.

The Broncos never did come close to figuring out the flex defense and all of the stunts and blitzes that go with it. Led by Too Mean Harvey Martin and Too Strong Randy White, the Cowboys' front four put so

much pressure on Morton that he set a Super Bowl record for interceptions (four) before the first half had even ended. By the middle of the third quarter, Morton was on the sidelines.

While the Cowboys defense was the dominant force in the game, Dallas was not without its celebrities on offense. Staubach had a fine day, hitting 19 passes out of 28 for 182 yards. And Butch Johnson made a diving catch of a Staubach bomb for a third-quarter touchdown that will have to go into the scrapbooks alongside Super Bowl catches by Max McGee, Lynn Swann and Fred Biletnikoff. "Roger told me to run a good post and the rest is history," said Butch. Someone said, "It looked spectacular." And Butch said, "It was."

However, members of the Dallas defense had more reason to talk than anyone else. Martin, who devoured Denver tackle Andy Maurer like so much barbecued shrimp, said, "He stopped me short in the first half, but I gave him some different looks and went inside on him a lot. Orange Crush is soda water, baby. You drink it. It don't win football games."

White, who dined on so many platters of Denver guard Tom Glassic on the half shell, said, "We knew pressuring Craig was the key and it was all on our shoulders. We wanted it." And then there was the gesturing Henderson, who added, "I'm sorry they took Morton out. I wanted him to throw me a couple."

One had to feel sorrow for Morton, who was also a Super Bowl loser as the Cowboys quarterback in 1971. He was a good friend of many of his Sunday enemies, and he and Roger Staubach had even hugged one another after the opening flip of the coin. Dallas won that too. ★

POSTSCRIPT *Randy White and Harvey Martin were named co–MVPs of the game. Only six other defensive players have been named Super Bowl MVP and two of those were also Cowboys: Chuck Howley (Super Bowl V) and Larry Brown (Super Bowl XXX).*

★ *White (54) and Martin basked in the Super glow after leading a ferocious pass rush that humiliated a former Cowboys quarterback.*

Excerpted from SPORTS ILLUSTRATED *January 23, 1978*

WALTER IOOSS JR.

THE 1970s TEXAS STYLE

★ *Upstart Southwest Airlines dressed its flight attendants in hot pants and go-go boots. The promotional tagline: "Long legs and short nights."*

EVERYONE ON THE TEAM SCORES WHEN HER POM-POMS FLY!

DEBBIE DOES DALLAS

starring **BAMBI WOODS** with MISTY WINTER · PAT ALLURE · ROBYN BYRD · RIKKI O'NEAL ARCADIA LAKE · PAULA HEAD · GEORGETTE SANDERS · RICHARD BALLA Produced & Directed by JIM CLARK Director of Photography BILLY BUDD Written by MARIA MINESTRA · Production Supervisor DEXTER EAGLE

"Wait till you see the weird part."

NORTH DALLAS FORTY

★ *The Cowboys' image took a double hit with the film version of Peter Gent's novel and a porn classic.*

Bambi Woods, star of *Debbie Does Dallas*, claimed she once tried out to be a Dallas Cowboys Cheerleader. She didn't make it.

★ *The real cowboy of the Cowboys, Walt Garrison wrestled steers on the pro rodeo circuit in the off-season.*

★ *Hitting legend Ted Williams, the first manager of the new 1972 Texas Rangers, went 54–100 in his lone season in Texas.*

★ *Howard Cosell and Don Meredith famously teamed up on* Monday Night Football; *the game was deemed won when Dandy Don sang, "Turn out the lights, the party's over. . . . "*

★ *Speedster Bob Hayes climbed into a cockpit in his own version of a flight suit, vintage 1973.*

★ *Tom Landry was strictly a coat-and-tie man for Sunday games, but he dressed down to oh-so-tight shorts at practice.*

★ *The Ewings of* Dallas *debuted in 1978, and scandalized TV for 14 seasons.*

THE 1970s IN PICTURES

HEINZ KLUETMEIER (2)

★ *Throughout his career Roger Staubach had the benefit of working behind the hugely talented OT Rayfield Wright, a Hall of Famer.*
★ *A menacing Harvey Martin crashed on Rams QB James Harris in the Jan. '76 NFC title game; the Cowboys dominated, 37–7.*

★ *Off the field and out of the spotlight, the Dallas
Cowboys Cheerleaders, 1978 vintage, took a breather.*

★ *The original cheerleaders, the Cow Belles, cheered in the Cowboys
first Super Bowl, in 1971; in '72, the new-look girls took over.*

★ *Mike Ditka (89) had four seasons as a Cowboys tight end, then became an assistant coach in Dallas before moving on to coach the Bears.*
★ *Even Tom Landry got excited on occasion, as in Super Bowl X against Pittsburgh. In headset, relatively calm, is assistant Dan Reeves.*

★ *Never shy, Thomas "Hollywood" Henderson taunted the Rams on an interception return for a TD in a 28–0 NFC title game win in '79.*
★ *Bob Lilly put the heat on during the Cowboys' first Super Bowl, in January 1971, won by the Colts on a last-minute field goal.*

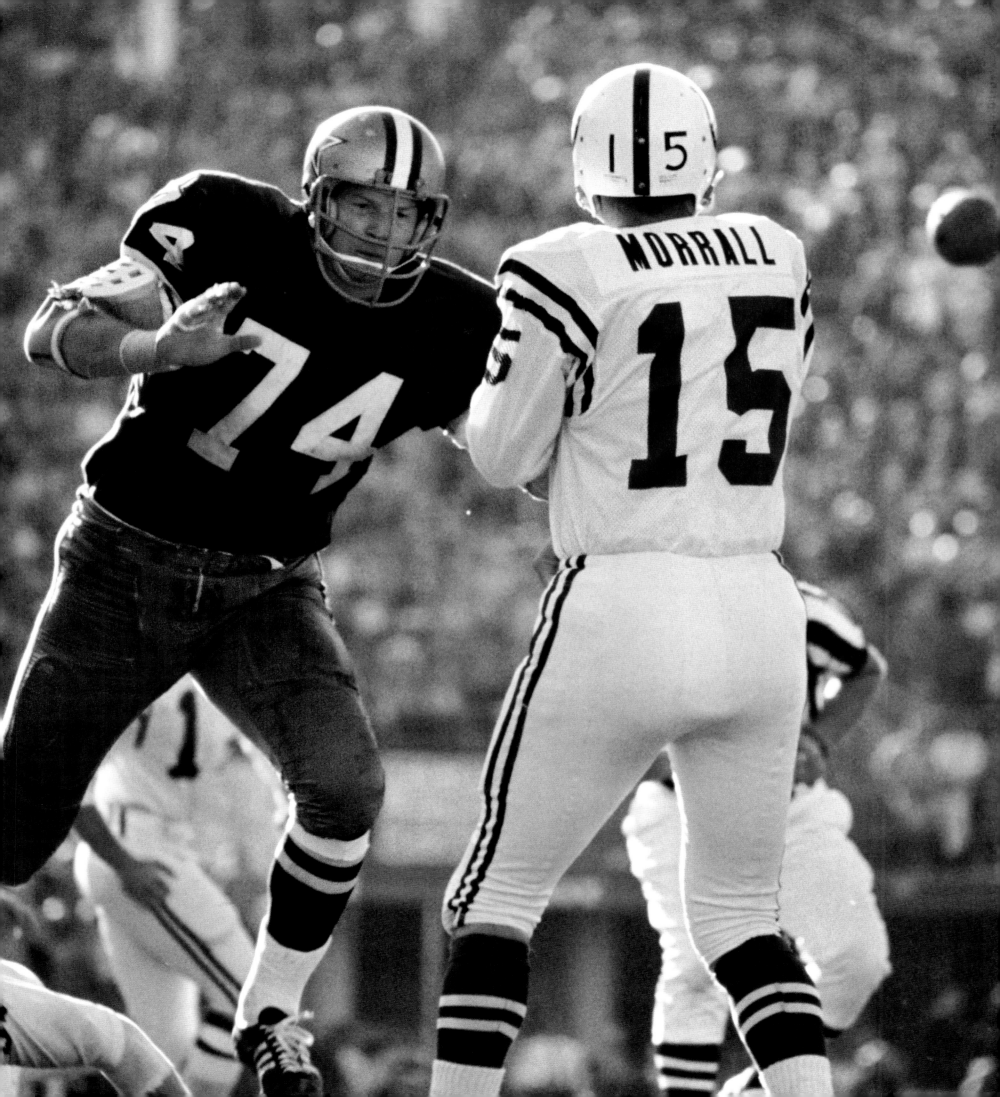

★ Middle linebacker Lee Roy Jordan (55) was the on-field director—as well as the inspirational leader—of the famed "Doomsday Defense."
★ In the '77 season, Harvey Martin set a still-standing club record for sacks with 23, and holds the Cowboys alltime career mark with 114.

★ *Over 13 seasons in Dallas, six-time Pro Bowl linebacker Chuck Howley (54) was a defensive mainstay and a Tom Landry favorite.*
★ *Drew Pearson scored early in Super Bowl X, a classic won by the Steelers, 21–17, after the teams combined for 21 fourth-quarter points.*

★ *Safety Cliff Harris ("Captain Crash") went undrafted out of tiny Ouachita Baptist University, but blossomed into a perennial All-Pro.*
★ *The sullen Cowboy enigma, Duane Thomas flashed his skills in the Super Bowl V loss; a year later, in SB VI, he would be a star.*

★ *A renowned scrambler, dubbed "Roger the Dodger" in college at Navy, Staubach eluded the Steelers' Dwight White in Super Bowl X.*
★ *Both world-class sprinters in college, DB Mel Renfro and WR Bob Hayes stopped to consult in Super Bowl V at the Orange Bowl.*

★ Bob Lilly, the first Cowboy inducted into the Hall of Fame, bore down on 49er John Brodie in an NFC title game win in Jan. '72.

(FROM LEFT) WALTER IOOSS JR., HEINZ KLUETMEIER

★ After Super Bowl XII, Thomas (Hollywood) Henderson offered his opinion of the Broncos' "Orange Crush" defense.

1970s: THE ROUNDUP

★ ALL-DECADE TEAM ★

OFFENSE

QB ★ ROGER STAUBACH (1969–79)

RB ★ TONY DORSETT (1977–87)

FB ★ ROBERT NEWHOUSE (1972–83)

WR ★ DREW PEARSON (1973–83)

WR ★ BOB HAYES (1965–74)

TE ★ BILLY JOE DuPREE (1973–83)

T ★ RAYFIELD WRIGHT (1967–79)

G ★ TOM RAFFERTY (1976–89)

C ★ JOHN FITZGERALD (1971–80)

G ★ BLAINE NYE (1968–76)

T ★ RALPH NEELY (1965–77)

K ★ TONI FRITSCH (1971–73, '75)

RET ★ BUTCH JOHNSON (1976–83)

DEFENSE

DE ★ HARVEY MARTIN (1973–83)

DT ★ RANDY WHITE (1975–88)

DT ★ JETHRO PUGH (1965–78)

DE ★ ED JONES (1974–78, '80–89)

LB ★ THOMAS HENDERSON (1975–79)

LB ★ D.D. LEWIS (1968, 1970-81)

LB ★ LEE ROY JORDAN (1963–76)

DB ★ CLIFF HARRIS (1970–79)

DB ★ CHARLIE WATERS (1970–78, '80-81)

DB ★ BENNY BARNES (1972–82)

DB ★ MEL RENFRO (1964–77)

P ★ DANNY WHITE (1976–88)

COACH ★ TOM LANDRY (1960–88)

BEST DRAFT SURPRISE

DENNIS THURMAN DB USC ▶
Drafted 11th round, 1978, 306th overall

Though a two-time All-America for the Trojans, Thurman was the 44th defensive back picked—which proved to be Dallas's good fortune. In 121 games as a Cowboy over eight seasons, Thurman intercepted 36 passes and ascended to the captaincy of the defensive backfield; he never missed a game to injury in his pro career.

BIGGEST DRAFT BUST

BILL THOMAS RB BOSTON COLLEGE
Drafted 1st round, 1972, 26th overall

Thomas's ill-fated career began in a hospital bed, as he recovered from shoulder surgery. He was waived in '73 with just two kickoff returns—and no carries—as a Cowboy. (Nine picks after selecting Thomas, Dallas took RB Robert Newhouse out of the University of Houston, who would ultimately make amends for the Thomas pick.)

★ A COWBOY TO REMEMBER *TE Jackie Smith played 15 Hall of Fame seasons in St. Louis but is best known for dropping a sure TD pass as a Cowboy in SB XIII.*

★ *Dallas bigwig: Still a receiver for the Cowboys in '73, Bob Hayes moonlighted as sales director for the Consolidated Wig Corporation.*

> BY THE NUMBERS

35 | Million dollars to build Texas Stadium in Irving, opened during the 1971 season. The cost of the project was paid entirely with private funds secured by owner Clint Murchison Jr.

10 | Pro Bowl appearances for defensive back Mel Renfro who was honored in each of his first 10 seasons in the league, selected as a free safety from 1964 through '69 and as a cornerback from 1970 through '73.

176 | Scoring differential during the 1978 season. Dallas's offense scored a league-high 384 points; its defense gave up an NFC-low 208.

23 | Sacks by Harvey Martin in 1977, five years before the official recognition of the statistic. The current NFL record of 22½ is held by the New York Giants' Michael Strahan.

1 | NFL coach, Tom Landry, to head both a winless team (0-11-1 in 1960) as well as a Super Bowl championship squad (1971, '77 seasons).

9 | Career postseason interceptions by DB Charlie Waters who set the still-standing NFL record in 1979 (since tied by Bill Simpson and Ronnie Lott).

GOLDEN RICHARDS, MARCH 1973
The Cowboys newly drafted (second-round pick) wide receiver when he was asked where he got the name Golden:

" **My mother and father gave it to me.** "

OVERLOOKED GAME OF THE DECADE

DECEMBER 23, 1972 AT SAN FRANCISCO Trailing 28–16 with just 2:02 remaining in the NFC divisional playoff, Roger Staubach, who had relieved starter Craig Morton earlier in the half, threw a 20-yard scoring pass to Billy Parks. Dallas recovered the ensuing onside kick and less than a minute later, Staubach found Ron Sellers from 10 yards out for the deciding TD in an improbable 30–28 win. To Staubach's great dismay, Tom Landry chose Morton to start the next game, a 26–3 loss to the Redskins for the NFC title.

WHAT WERE THEY THINKING?

ON JUNE 20, 1979, in the prime of his NFL career, Ed (Too Tall) Jones, 28, stunned the Cowboys by announcing that he was leaving football to pursue professional boxing. "I've never liked football," he declared. "It's a sport I was forced into." Against heavyweights of dubious quality, Too Tall did earn a 6–0 record; the Cowboys, meanwhile, were forced to start an aging Larry Cole in his place. Having apparently satisfied his jones for pugilism after a year in the ring, Too Tall returned to the Cowboys in 1980 for 10 more productive seasons.

★ IT'S A FACT: *On Jan. 3, 1970 the Cowboys played in the last-ever NFL "Playoff Bowl" game, a.k.a. the Runner-Up Bowl, losing 31–0 to the Rams.*

The ★ 19

In a decade erupting in management turnover,

80s

★ JOHNSON ★   ★ WHITE ★   ★ DORSETT ★   ★ WHITE ★   ★ WALKER ★

the Cowboys produced lots of drama—but no titles

Randy White, the rock of the Dallas defense in the '80s and on his way to the Pro Football Hall of Fame, drew a bead on Redskins QB Joe Theismann.

1981

HOW TO BE A REAL COWBOY

FOR FOUR YEARS, TONY DORSETT DIDN'T QUITE FIT IN DALLAS. BUT THAT CHANGED

BY RICK TELANDER

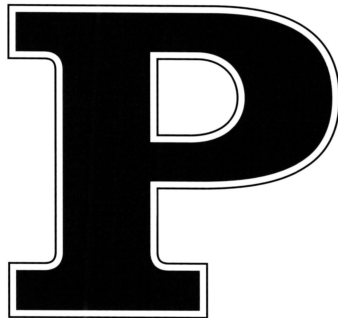

ETE GENT IS THERE, IN THE second row, looking troubled. In front of him sits Don Meredith, long-jawed, half-hayseed, smiling like a sharp. Don Perkins is there, too, and Bob Hayes and Dan Reeves. Way in the back looms big Bob Lilly. Nobody seems to know how the 1965 Dallas Cowboys team photo made its way onto the locker room bulletin board. But there it is. And as the players trickle out, most stop to look at the old-timers. ★ Tony Dorsett walks up and puts a finger on the photo, looking up at the faces and then down at the names listed below. "Don Perkins," he says softly. "Renfro." His eyes move to the grimacing young man sitting in the second row, the one who looks upset, betrayed somehow, as though the sun is shining in his eyes only. ★ "Pete Gent?" asks Dorsett. It is Gent, a Cowboy receiver from 1964 to 1968, the player who fell out with

Excerpted from
SPORTS ILLUSTRATED
December 7, 1981

★ *Small for a running back at 5' 10", 188 pounds, Dorsett thrived on an uncanny instinct for avoiding tacklers.*

The Cowboys' System and later wrote his indictment of it, *North Dallas Forty*. There have been other name players who fell out—Pat Toomay, Duane Thomas, Hollywood Henderson; The System doesn't even tolerate sitting on the fence—but Gent is probably the best known and most thoughtful of them, the outcasts, the Men Who Didn't Fit.

If there is tension in Dorsett as he gazes at the photo, it is because until recently he seemed to be falling out too. Though he routinely gained a thousand yards a year for the Cowboys, Dorsett didn't have that something—obedience, perhaps—that let Dallasites know where he stood, whether or not he was a real company man. Early along he did that uncool stuff—got into a bar fight, changed the pronunciation of his name from DOR-sett to Dor-SETT (which is how a buddy said they said it in France), told folks he'd be quitting football after five years to go into acting full time, had "TD" painted on the doors of his Lincoln Continental.

Dallas fans, described by Gil Brandt, the vice-president for personnel development, as "a white-collar, discerning audience," cheered players like Randy White and Harvey Martin. But they showered Dorsett with ambivalence. In 1978 Dorsett's parents flew in from the family hometown, Aliquippa, Pa., to watch a game. Dorsett had missed a practice earlier that week and been fined, and when he entered the game, the crowd at Texas Stadium heartily booed. It was a bad scene.

And then, last spring, things changed abruptly, amazingly. Dorsett got married. He gave up his apartment in town and with his wife, Julie, and her 5-year-old daughter, Shukura, moved into a house 21 miles northeast of Dallas. He stayed out of bars; he worked out furiously; he showed up for camp last July in perfect shape. Tom Landry took one look and named Dorsett a team captain. The hottest items on Dallas sports pages became "New Tony Dorsett" stories. He seemed happy enough, and yet there was something almost grim about the 27-year-old's determination, his measured speech, his avoidance of controversy. He has maintained that attitude this season, and no doubt as a result is having his best year ever, with 1,331 yards rushing, 5.0 yards per carry. What happened?

"You hope in this life that you grow and don't always repeat your mistakes," Dorsett says, turning from the 1965 team picture. "I'm in the best shape physically and mentally I've ever been in and I don't

"TONY IS SHY. From the start people here misunderstood him. He got labeled a troublemaker—which he certainly isn't—and it's hard to get rid of that."

want to waste anything now. I've made adjustments." He shrugs. "I mean, I guess I've matured."

As Dorsett walks blank-faced across the parking lot, it's clear that Pete Gent is no longer on his mind.

IF YOU WANT ONE PLAY THAT best illustrates what Tony Dorsett can do on a football field, you could go with a run he made off left tackle last year against St. Louis. The ball was on the Cardinals' four-yard line. The right defensive end was crashing down, the right linebacker was filling, the two corners were blitzing, and Dorsett was heading full steam into what was essentially a cup of defenders. Suddenly he pivoted on his right foot and stepped straight back out of the hole, turning 360 degrees. The two corners, Roger Wehrli and Carl Allen, collided headfirst at the exact spot where Dorsett had been an instant before. Dorsett swung wide around the left end, and though hemmed in by the safety, somehow outran him for a touchdown. The play lasted only a few seconds, but during it five defenders knew they were going to tackle Dorsett, yet none of them even *touched* him.

Dorsett speaks often of seeing "flashes of color" when he runs, blips of enemy hue that steer him through trouble like warning lights. On that play, though, he doesn't know what he saw. "It wasn't even color flashes," he says. "Sometimes it's just this feeling for everything that's happening around you, almost like an outside force. I knew people were coming and I stepped back in a spin . . . and . . . it was incredible." He stops there, humbled by the memory.

The Cowboys, as everyone knows, have tests for everything. They have a drill developed by conditioning coach Dr. Bob Ward, called the Agility-Speed-Unexpected Vi-

sual Stimulus Test, which uses flashing lights to direct runners in various directions. No one has come close to Dorsett's score. As Ward says, "His ability to perceive the unexpected is extraordinary."

On the surface everything has gone splendidly for Dorsett all along. In Dallas he started right off with the endorsements for Converse and 7-Up. His football contract, renewed last season, was for six figures. The girls were always there. In a 1979 Gallup survey, American teenagers voted Dorsett their second favorite sports personality. First choice was near-saint Roger Staubach.

The problem was that although Dorsett was an adult, he was reluctant to put away youthful things. A lot of it was friskiness, just plain I'm-rich-and-happy

★ *Dorsett's move to a home in far suburbia was part of his maturing process, but when in need of a thrill, he had his wheels.*

exuberance: the stories about acting ("No, I don't think I want to act," he says now), the time he and a date were taken to jail in handcuffs (because Dorsett didn't think the cops were acting civilly toward them), the vanity license plates that read TD 33. ("I got rid of those fast," he says.)

"Tony is shy to a degree," says his good friend, cornerback Dennis Thurman. "And from the start people here misunderstood him. Realistically, having that much money and coming from where he did, well, he needed time to adjust. But he got labeled a troublemaker—which he certainly isn't—and it's hard to get rid of that. He was always accepted by the players. But it's only now that he's acting the way outside people expected from Day One."

At halftime of the Dallas-Miami game earlier this season, Mel Renfro walked onto the field to be inducted into the Cowboys' Ring of Honor. Tony Dorsett remembers feeling very happy for Renfro at this moment (they were teammates in 1977), but not thinking of his own chances of being similarly honored by the Cowboys. If things continue as they have, though, Dorsett is a shoe-in for the Ring. He is already the best running back in Cowboys history. Though the criteria for being selected aren't precise, being a good and loyal Cowboy clearly is important. When asked earlier how or why or when a player is chosen for the Ring, Tex Schramm, the Cowboys' president and general manager, shot back, "The organization decides."

Dorsett sits now at a table in the party room in his house, out there on the plains where people tether horses in their backyards. (Dorsett fell while riding a horse a couple of years ago and these days prefers to charge around the countryside on his Kawasaki 750.) The room features a huge stereo, a bar, a trophy or two, and Dallas-blue and silver decorations. Dorsett had it done this way and calls it his "Cowboy Room."

He discusses the changes he is now going through. "People can say, 'You can't buck the system,' right? 'Perform or leave,' right? But a lot of it is realizing what your role is. I've found I can do certain things and still remain me. With friends, my wife and I can be ourselves; with diplomatic people, we can be diplomatic. Now I know you've got to be versatile in life." ★

POSTSCRIPT *Dorsett would finish the '81 season with 1,646 rushing yards, his career best. On Oct. 9, 1994 in a halftime ceremony at Texas Stadium, he was inducted into the Ring of Honor.*

1982

STILL STANDING AT THE TOP

THE DALLAS POWER STRUCTURE: FOUR MEN WITH LITTLE IN COMMON—EXCEPT WINNING

BY WILLIAM OSCAR JOHNSON

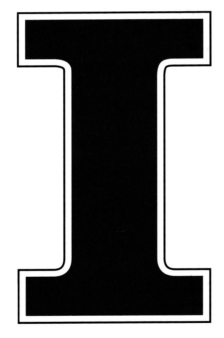

Excerpted from
SPORTS ILLUSTRATED
September 1, 1982

IT IS 22 YEARS SINCE THE DALLAS Cowboys first appeared in the NFL—as sorry a bunch of football players as ever heard themselves booed in a half-empty home stadium. In that bright and innocent autumn of 1960, Y.A. Tittle was in his prime, Jack Kennedy had just beaten Richard Nixon for the presidency, the Beatles were still in their teens, and the Cowboys were 0-11-1. ★ However, that single tie, a 31–31 game with the Giants in New York on Dec. 4, offered some small reason for celebration, and Clint Murchison Jr., the wry, diminutive Texas Croesus whose fortune had bought, bred and fed those hapless Cowboys, recently spoke of it with fondness: "I remember well that day when we failed to lose our first game." ★ The Cowboys didn't fail to lose many more games in the next five years. By the end of the 1965 season their total record was 25-53-4. However, a 7–7 mark in 1965 was the turnaround. Not once

★ *The original Cowboy brain trust—Landry, Schramm, Brandt and Murchison—proved enduring.*

in the last 16 seasons have they lost more than they have won. And, incredibly, today Dallas has the winningest regular-season record in the NFL for the '60s, '70s and '80s. And, whereas other winning clubs have experienced streaks and spurts of goodness or greatness, Dallas has been almost supernally consistent, missing the playoffs only once in those 16 years since '65 and playing in five Super Bowls—winning two of them, six years apart with two almost totally different teams.

So what does this mean? Well, for one thing, it means that an aura of myth—or miracle—has grown up around something called The Dallas Organization. People speak with awe of this thing—as if it were a cathedral or a shrine where one can go to be cured of everything from lumbago to losing poker hands. *The Dallas Organization.* It sounds monolithic, grandiose, like IBM, the Mafia, the Ewings or the Pentagon. Over the years, serious analysts of corporate structure have asked the Cowboys to share with them their managerial formula, the charts and diagrams that explain their administrative process. The Cowboys have had to say no.

For, in fact, The Dallas Organization is way too simple, way too small, for such an analysis. As a business the Cowboys are more akin to a mom-and-pop gas station than they are to General Motors. The Dallas Organization is nothing more than the tenuous chemistry that exists in the relationship of three men who share credit equally for making The Organization what it is, plus a fourth who operates at a slightly lower level of influence and responsibility.

The handful of men who occupy the minuscule peak of this tiny corporate pyramid do not operate as a palsy-walsy little committee either. Each has his own well-defined bailiwick, and there is a minimum of contact among them of any nature—particularly of a social nature. This is because they are totally improbable partners or colleagues in any kind of undertaking, be it business or pleasure. The following thumbnail sketches of The Dallas Organization principals will make it plain exactly how odd this odd-couple-times-two really is:

The owner and board chairman, Clint Williams Murchison Jr., 58, is very unlike the caricature of a Texas zillionaire. He's extremely articulate, humorous, curious, bright, with a masters from the Massachusetts Institute of Technology—a theoretical mathematician, no less, and a damned good one. He has an almost elfin look, with horn-rimmed spectacles and a gray, clipped, flattop haircut. He's a

multimillionaire and the son of one, an oil baron. For most of his years, Clint Jr. walked on the flamboyant side, enjoying good companions, good times, good booze. In one of the few recorded incidents of nonbusiness fraternizing among the hierarchy of The Organization, Clint married Gil Brandt's ex-wife, Anne, in 1975. Since then she has undergone a born-again Christian experience. So has Clint, and the impact of this religious commitment has pretty much undercut his penchant for fun living.

The president and general manager, Texas Ernest Schramm, 62, has decidedly not undergone a religious conversion. He is a hail-fellow type, given to Scotch, laughter, tale spinning and terrible tirades—usually directed at the officials—mixed with unbut-

★ *The Dallas Cowboys Cheerleaders were invented in 1972 by the showman Schramm—but detested by the moralist Landry.*

toned hurrahs in the press box. Schramm grew up in Los Angeles but went to the University of Texas because his stockbroker father, who had named his only son after his native state, wanted some of the Lone Star magic to rub off on him. Schramm majored in journalism, went to work as sports editor of an Austin paper, then happily returned home in 1947, when the Los Angeles Rams hired him as a public relations man. He's a born impresario, someone who loves the flash and fun of the showbiz side of the game. He invented the strutting, swiveling chorus line of the Dallas cheerleaders, among other things. He's a man of great passion, restless innovation and powerful loyalties.

The head coach, Thomas Wade Landry, 57, may look like a granite effigy on the sidelines, but that's misleading, for he's a gracious, pleasant fellow in conversation. Not humorous, however, and decidedly not a backslapper and not a cusser or a drinker. Indeed, in the same undramatic, casual tone that another man will use to tell you what he does for a living, Tom will say to you, "The number 1 factor in my life is my relationship to God." He wrote in a newspaper article that he talks to God regularly. Landry is concerned about the incipient immorality in the U.S. these days, as manifested on TV and in films. He has always believed that the Dallas cheerleaders are an indisputable—if minor—reflection of that problem. He doesn't approve of their presence on his sidelines. He also didn't like the Cowboys being labeled "America's Team"—a sobriquet that was one of two titles that NFL Films offered Schramm as the billboard for the Cowboys' 1978 highlights film. Landry says, "I think that title gave us a lot more trouble than it was worth. The other teams resented us for it."

The vice president of personnel development, Gilbert Harvey Brandt, 49, was working as a baby photographer in Milwaukee when Schramm asked him to help out signing players for the still nonexistent Dallas team in the fall of 1959. Brandt's hobby as a University of Wisconsin physical education major was studying college game films to see why some players were better than others. Schramm had first heard of Brandt from one of his players in L.A., Elroy (Crazylegs) Hirsch, the Wisconsin halfback who starred as an end for the Rams. Brandt heads the Cowboys' nine-man scouting staff. He's an odd combination of computer memory bank and traveling salesman. He pores over the intricacies of readouts, evaluating potential Cowboy draftees like a medi-

 THE MEN WHO occupy the minuscule peak of this tiny corporate pyramid do not operate as a palsy-walsy committee. They are totally improbable partners.

eval monk studying a Latin text, yet in his other life he's a born glad-hander. He sees to it that Cowboy birthday cards are sent to the sons and daughters of every significant coach in America. In coaching circles, he's known for his Cowboy-style high-on-the-hog hospitality. He's always on the sidelines for Cowboys games—as much for the public relations value of being seen on TV as anything else.

So these diverse, divergent personalities are The Dallas Organization, and because of them the dynamo hums, the computers whir and the Cowboys win and win and win. What's the secret? Brains? Religion? Money? Longevity? Luck? Cunning? Salesmanship?

Well, it's some of all of that, but mainly, The Organization is nothing more than a happy cosmic coincidence. As Murchison says, "Another year, another group of people with slightly different backgrounds, and none of this would have happened."

How much longer can it last? What happens when the magical chemistry is dissolved? Who knows? Murchison says, "Maybe the momentum will continue for a few years. Maybe not. But we'll find out fairly soon. Tom is 57, Tex is 62 and I'm 58. Though we keep searching, none of us has found the Fountain of Youth." ★

POSTSCRIPT *Murchison may have had a premonition, for the magic did not last much longer. Less than two years later, in 1984, Murchison, in failing health, sold the Cowboys to an investment syndicate led by H.R. "Bum" Bright, a Dallas businessman. When Bright sold the team to Jerry Jones in February 1989, Jones fired Landry, to the shock of most everyone. Brandt was fired after the draft that year. Soon after, Schramm resigned. From the time this story appeared until Jones's purchase of the team, the Cowboys' record was only 56–53, including 3–13 in Landry's final season.*

1989

THE NEW GUY GETS BUSY

PREPPING FOR HIS FIRST SEASON AS THE COWBOYS HEAD COACH, JIMMY JOHNSON STAYED UP LATE

BY PAUL ZIMMERMAN

JIMMY JOHNSON, THE NEW coach of the Dallas Cowboys, rises from his table in the little Italian joint around the corner from the Cowboys' training center, and the bar comes alive. Everyone in the place has been sneaking peeks at this chubby guy from Port Arthur, Texas, who made a name for himself at the University of Miami before replacing a legend, Tom Landry. What did he eat? Caesar salad and stuffed eggplant. Hmmm. And drink? A Heineken over ice. Must be some kind of Miami thing.

He's wearing a dark pin-striped suit, a white shirt with blue stripes and a conservative red tie—banker's clothes. Everyone checks the carefully groomed hair, the hair that was the subject of so many one-liners when the press and everyone else in town was lashing out in anger over the way Landry got dumped on Feb. 25, right after oilman Jerry Jones, who was Johnson's roommate and teammate at Arkansas, bought the Cowboys for a reported $140 million. Johnson has a ruddy, almost jolly-looking face, but the eyes are hard and penetrating.

Now Johnson is ready to leave, and the whoopees start.

"We're with you, Jimmy!"

"Give 'em hell, Jimmy!"

Then softer and grumpier, an old-timer's voice: "Just win more than three, Jimmy."

He can probably do that next fall, but don't expect a playoff season or even a winning record from the 1989 Cowboys. "There are no quick fixes," says Dallas's former offensive coordinator Paul Hackett. "You could see 10 to 15 new faces on that football team."

Johnson has been on the job for less than three weeks. He has had his meals sent in to his office. He has been out to eat twice—at the Italian joint. Home is a condo rented by the team, 3½ blocks from the Cowboys' complex. His wife, Linda Kay, and their two boys are in Miami, where she is trying to sell a house the family bought just seven months ago.

His staff consists of six of his assistants from the University of Miami, four Cowboy holdovers, offensive coordinator David Shula, who was brought in from the Miami Dolphins, and quarterback coach Jerry Rhome, who was with the San Diego Chargers. They have been working late and on weekends, trying to learn the personnel, breaking down game tapes. "You know, one of the Dallas people told me the previous coaching staff went home for dinner every night during the season—every night," says Johnson.

And his staff? "C'mon now," he says.

Where does he start as he attempts to cure the sick dog that was the 3–13 Cowboys? How long will it take? Says Johnson, "It would be premature of me to sit here and say it will take such and such amount of time. Obviously, the key is personnel. This draft is probably the most important one I'll ever have in the NFL. We pick first. I want to be in a position where, in three years, I can say we had a great draft." ★

POSTSCRIPT *A month later, in that first draft, Johnson selected quarterback Troy Aikman (UCLA) with the top pick. In the second round he took fullback Daryl Johnston (Syracuse); in the third round, center Mark Stepnoski (Pitt); and in the fourth round, defensive end Tony Tolbert (Texas–El Paso). All would come to play prominent roles with the Cowboys. The team would finish 1–15 in Johnson's first season, but in the ensuing draft, Johnson used the 17th pick of the first round to select a running back from Florida named Emmitt Smith. And the rest, you might say, is Super Bowl history.*

★ *Besides getting up to speed with his staff, the well-groomed Johnson was preparing for the critically important NFL draft.*

Excerpted from SPORTS ILLUSTRATED *March 20, 1989*

THE 1980s TEXAS STYLE

★ Former movie cowboy Ronald Reagan and Texas's own George Bush ruled the '80s political stage.

★ The sensational Eric Dickerson led SMU to an undefeated season in 1982. Five years later the NCAA slapped the school with the infamous "death penalty" for paying players.

★ The State Fair pig races launched in '86—on a track known as Pork Chop Downs.

★ The Cowboys Cheerleaders became a commercial bonanza, from made-for-TV movies to shampoo ads.

Charles Durning was an Oscar nominee as Best Supporting Actor for his role as "the Governor" in *The Best Little Whorehouse in Texas.*

★ *Burt Reynolds and Dolly Parton lit up the screen, bringing fame to the real-life (long gone) Chicken Ranch in La Grange.*

With Burt and Dolly this much fun just couldn't be legal!

THE BEST LITTLE WHOREHOUSE IN TEXAS

★ *John Travolta was the style cowboy of the decade, preening in the movie Urban Cowboy.*

★ *Barney was born in Dallas in '87, the purple brainchild of Sheryl Leach.*

THE 1980s IN PICTURES

★ The usually vivacious Harvey Martin had his game face on during a 26–10 victory over the archrival Redskins in 1981.

★ QB Danny White's name dots the Cowboys record book, but he was frequently frustrated by failures in the postseason.

★ In a 30–17 postseason win over Tampa Bay in January '83, TE Doug Cosbie, a future Pro Bowler, cheered a Ron Springs touchdown.
★ In the stark sun and shadow created by the hole in the roof at Texas Stadium, Mike Renfro scored in a 1984 loss to the Redskins.

★ *In a pregame chalk talk during the 1981 season, Tom Landry had a few late details to pass along to a banged-up Tony Dorsett.*
★ *Of Dorsett's many shining achievements, the most brilliant and memorable was an NFL–record 99-yard run against the Vikings in '83.*

★ A potent D, with left tackle John Dutton (78) and left end Ed Jones (72), led Dallas to the playoffs after the strike-shortened '82 season.
★ Bitter nemeses whenever they faced each other, the Cowboys fell to the Redskins, 31–17, in the NFC title game in January '83.

★ Ed Jones, most always known as "Too Tall," was too much for Atlanta's Chris Miller in '89, the last of Too Tall's 15 Cowboy seasons.
★ Among Dorsett's gifts was an instinct for seeing gaps and changing direction, as here in a January '86 playoff game with the Rams.

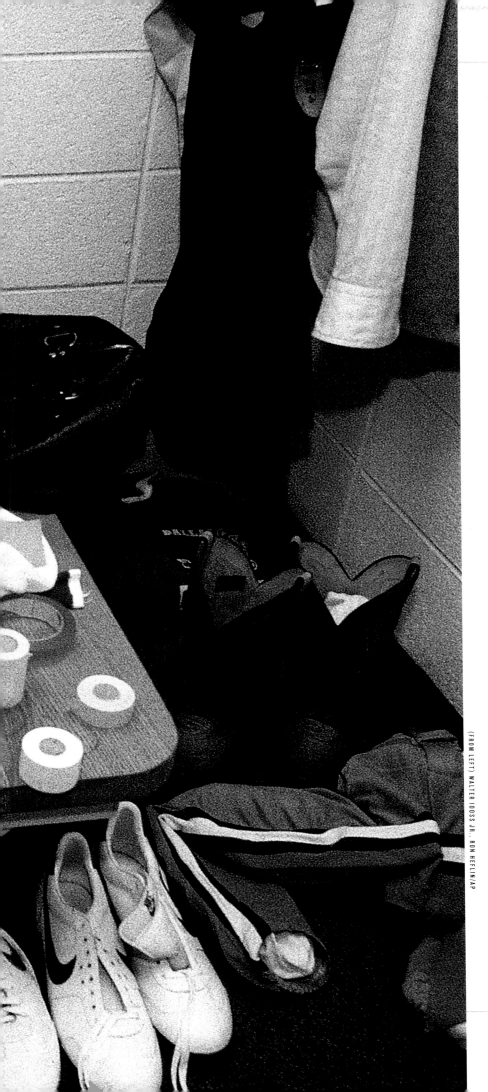

★ Perhaps dreaming of victory, Harvey Martin took a pregame
snooze in the visitors locker room in Philly in '81; Dallas won, 17–14.

★ Herschel Walker, in efficient headgear, prepared for the '88
season; it would be his career best, with over 1,500 yards rushing.

1980s: The Roundup

★ ALL-DECADE TEAM ★

OFFENSE

QB ★ DANNY WHITE (1976–88)

RB ★ TONY DORSETT (1977–87)

FB ★ RON SPRINGS (1979–84)

WR ★ TONY HILL (1977–86)

WR ★ DREW PEARSON (1973–83)

TE ★ DOUG COSBIE (1979–88)

T ★ HERB SCOTT (1975–84)

G ★ KURT PETERSEN (1980–85)

C ★ TOM RAFFERTY (1976–89)

G ★ NATE NEWTON (1986–98)

T ★ JIM COOPER (1977–86)

K ★ RAFAEL SEPTIEN (1978–86)

RET ★ JAMES JONES (1980–85)

DEFENSE

DE ★ JIM JEFFCOAT (1983–94)

DT ★ JOHN DUTTON (1979–86)

DT ★ RANDY WHITE (1975–88)

DE ★ ED JONES (1974–78, '80–89)

LB ★ MIKE HEGMAN (1976–88)

LB ★ EUGENE LOCKHART (1984–90)

LB ★ BOB BREUNIG (1975–84)

DB ★ EVERSON WALLS (1981–89)

DB ★ DENNIS THURMAN (1978–85)

DB ★ DEXTOR CLINKSCALE (1980, '82–85)

DB ★ MICHAEL DOWNS (1981–88)

P ★ MIKE SAXON (1985–92)

COACH ★ TOM LANDRY (1960–88)

BEST DRAFT SURPRISE

CHAD HENNINGS DT AIR FORCE ▶
Drafted 11th round, 1988, 290th overall

Tex Schramm again saw past a four-year military commitment (a la Roger Staubach at Navy) to take a chance on budding pilot and Outland Trophy winner Chad Hennings. After flying air support missions over Iraq, Hennings played nine seasons in Dallas, collecting 27½ sacks and three Super Bowl rings.

BIGGEST DRAFT BUST

BILLY CANNON JR. LB TEXAS A&M
Drafted 1st round, 1984, 25th overall

Son of the 1959 Heisman Trophy winner, Cannon's pro career was cut short after just eight games by a spinal injury. After identifying a congenital spine defect, team doctors would not clear him to play for the '85 season. In '86 Cannon brought a $9.6 million negligence suit against the Cowboys; it was settled in '92.

★ A COWBOY TO REMEMBER *Safety Bill Bates's 217 games played rank second among all Cowboys; his bashing hits made him a 12-time All-Madden pick.*

★ *Yes, he's Too Tall: Making merry with his nickname, Ed Jones used all his 6 feet nine inches to taunt his not-tall-enough teammates.*

> BY THE NUMBERS

20 The Cowboys' NFL record for consecutive winning seasons starting in '66, ending in '86.

60 Million dollars, the price paid to Clint Murchison to purchase the Cowboys by a group headed by H.R. "Bum" Bright in 1984. Murchison, who had paid the NFL $600,000 for the original franchise in 1959, sold the team for a hundred times what he paid.

5 Years Bright owned the franchise before selling to Jerry Jones for a estimated $140 million. During Bright's tenure, the team had a record of 36–43.

28 Former or future Cowboys who played in the USFL, the most influential being Herschel Walker and Nate Newton.

44 Points, the largest margin of defeat in team history. Dallas lost 44–0 at Texas Stadium on Nov. 17, 1985 to the Chicago Bears, coached by former Cowboys tight end Mike Ditka (1969–72).

3 Times Dallas was shut out in 1989, the most times shut out in any season. In the franchise's 50-year history Dallas has been shut out a total of just 11 times. As a point of comparison, over that same time, the Chicago Bears have been shut out 30 times.

DEXTOR CLINKSCALE, DECEMBER 8, 1985
Cowboys safety, when he was asked if he ever dreamed Dallas could give up 44 and 50 points in two games in the same season:

" No, I dream about girls. "

OVERLOOKED GAME OF THE DECADE

OCTOBER 25, 1981 VS. DOLPHINS On the day retired All-Pro defender Mel Renfro was inducted into the Ring of Honor at Texas Stadium, it was offense that stole the spotlight as Dallas and Miami combined for 995 yards from scrimmage and 55 points. Trailing by 13 points with less than four minutes left in the fourth quarter, Danny White threw scoring strikes to tight end Doug Cosbie and fullback Ron Springs—sandwiched around a key interception by cornerback Dennis Thurman—to give Cowboys fans a hard-to-believe 28–27 victory.

WHAT WERE THEY THINKING?

DURING THE 57-DAY NFL PLAYERS STRIKE IN 1982, quarterback Danny White expressed his support for the owners, alienating a number of his teammates. For many the rift never healed, and after the 1983 season a group of Cowboys, saying White was unfit to lead them, called for coach Landry to turn to backup Gary Hogeboom to start the '84 season. Landry, citing a "feel" for his team, made Hogeboom the '84 starter. Ineffectiveness eventually landed Hogeboom back on the bench, and White returned to his starting role.

★ IT'S A FACT: *From Tom Landry's Dallas debut in 1960 until his dismissal in 1989, there were 187 head coaching changes in the NFL and AFL.*

The ★ 19

★ NEWTON ★　　★ WILLIAMS ★　　★ AIKMAN ★　　★ JOHNSON ★　　★ MARYLAND ★

Despite coaching trauma, the franchise returned

90s

★ JOHNSTON ★   ★ SWITZER ★   ★ IRVIN ★   ★ TUINEI ★   ★ SMITH ★

to glory on the wings of a powerful offense

★ *In a Jan. '94 thriller in New York, Emmitt Smith led Dallas to a 16–13 win in OT, launching the Cowboys toward a second straight Super Bowl title.*

1993

THE LOOK OF A DYNASTY

THE WAY THE YOUNG COWBOYS TRAMPLED BUFFALO SUGGESTED MUCH MORE TO COME

BY PAUL ZIMMERMAN

SUPER BOWL XXVII

Excerpted from
SPORTS ILLUSTRATED
February 8, 1993

GET USED TO THE DALLAS Cowboys, folks, because they're going to be with us for a long time. Here comes that dreaded word—*dynasty*. Oh, my, yes. Everything points to it after the Cowboys ran the Buffalo Bills out of the Rose Bowl on Sunday by a score of 52–17. Troy Aikman and Emmitt Smith and Michael Irvin and Ken Norton Jr. and Charles Haley—all those implements of destruction that embarrassed and humiliated a proud, battle-tested team are just starting to feel their oats. Coach Jimmy Johnson and his hair spray; Jerry Jones, the owner who hungers for the limelight. You say you're tired of them already? Gee, that's tough, because the whole gang's going to be with us for a while. ★ *Dynasty.* How we love that word. Seems that every time a new team

★ *Irvin caught a 19-yard TD pass in the second quarter and the confident Cowboys never looked back.*

JOHN BIEVER

wins a championship, in any sport, that word dynasty follows in lockstep. Only this time it makes sense, historical sense.

Chuck Noll was 1–13 in 1969, his first year as coach in Pittsburgh, and five years later his young Steelers had their first of four Super Bowl titles. The San Francisco 49ers were 2–14 under rookie coach Bill Walsh in '79, but in another two seasons they held the championship trophy, with three more Super Bowl victories to follow. Johnson and his Cowboys are right on course, a 1–15 record in his initial year, 1989, and now, three seasons later, a Super Bowl championship. And why does it look like only the beginning? Because youth defines this team.

You say that free agency could change everything, that the rules of the game are different now? Well, this is a game that Johnson, with his 46 trades in four seasons, and Jones, a guy who's ready to spend the bucks for talent, seem to have been born for.

"We don't know a specific way we'll be dealing with free agency," Jones said Sunday night. "But we'll figure it out. We'll sharpen our pencils. Don't think we can't figure it out. Somebody the other day told me I'd go through withdrawal this year because we don't have a lot of high draft choices. I told him, 'We don't have high picks yet, but wait until draft day.'"

Jones and Johnson—or, rather, Jerry and Jimmy—there's not another management team like it in the league. Two men make all the football decisions in Dallas; there's no vice president for pro personnel or director of player personnel to get in the way. Jones believes that if you make a mistake, make it going full-speed. "I've got a nice legal pad of failures in the business world," he said. "But I think whatever you do, you have to do it aggressively and tirelessly."

The first thing Jones did after he bought the team was hire Johnson, perhaps the only coach who could have matched him stride for stride. Johnson's achievement this season—in fact, over four seasons—has been remarkable, but as he went through the weeklong round of press conferences before the Super Bowl, you could sense a slight hesitancy by the press to treat him with the dignity that a Lombardi or a Tom Landry or even a Noll or a Joe Gibbs received.

During a press conference early in the week, Johnson was asked about the hair spray he uses. "I like to be neat," he said without batting an eye. "I'll admit to a little spray. I'm not a closet sprayer." Did anyone ever ask Don Shula about his jaw or Landry about

his hat or Lombardi about the way he puffed out his chest when he walked?

In one remarkable session with the media, on Jan. 27, Johnson stood on the rostrum and opened a slight window into the way he looks at his life by talking about a book that had influenced him, *Flow: The Psychology of Optimal Experience*. Then, as if he were reluctant to end the give-and-take, he sat at a table and kept talking with a handful of reporters, for 20, 30, 45 minutes, until the room started to empty. The reporters wanted to know how Johnson had come into

 SAID JOHNSON, "I like the guy who can walk into a poolroom and sink the 8 ball. The people I want around me, well, the bigger the game, the more they shine."

the NFL without any pro experience and put together exactly the type of team he wanted.

"I like the guy who can walk into a poolroom and pick up a cue stick and sink the 8 ball," said Johnson. "The people I want around me, well, the bigger the game, the more they shine. Some people, I don't care if it's a six-inch putt, when everything's on the line, it's very tough for them. It's the way their lives have been. I can't do a whole lot about it, just eliminate 'em from our program."

"You're lucky to have been hired by Jerry Jones," someone said, and Johnson's eyes got hard for a moment. "You just said a word I don't like or use—*luck*," he said. "There was nothing fortunate about it. I was one of the top coaches in college football. If I hadn't wound up here, I'd have been hired somewhere else."

Turnovers are the heart of most NFL blowouts, and the Bills will have to live with a Super Bowl–record nine as they analyze their third straight, and worst, defeat in the Big One. Two of the turnovers were returned for touchdowns. Three more set up TDs. Another one cut off a Buffalo drive in the end

zone. The other three were window dressing, including a 64-yard fumble return by 292-pound defensive tackle Leon Lett, who went into his hot-dog number a little early and had the ball knocked out of his hand just short of the end zone by Bills wide receiver Don Beebe. That was at the end, however, when the game was in its Laurel and Hardy phase and the fans were streaming out to beat the traffic.

As the clock wound down, the Cowboys were well into their victory celebration, whooping, hollering and dumping ice water on Johnson. Smith gave Johnson's hair a thorough massage. (Miraculously, it was back in place for the postgame award ceremony.) The 49-year-old Johnson had, in his first Super Bowl appearance, engineered the rout of a worthy opponent.

On Monday morning Johnson leaned forward inside the white stretch limousine that was taking him to the last Super Bowl press conference. "Hey," he said to those seated in the car with him, "were our players gunned up and ready to play yesterday or what? We have *players*. You know, while [Buffalo coach] Marv

★ Dallas captured a record nine turnovers, five resulting in touchdowns, in what Johnson gleefully dubbed a "feeding frenzy."

Levy is over there reading about Harry Truman, [Cowboy DT] Jimmie Jones is on his bed, belly-laughing at Fred and Barney on *The Flintstones*."

When the limo rolled up in front of the hotel, Johnson got out and met with Aikman in the lobby. The two of them rode down the escalator to the ballroom together. "Did I tell you about the turnovers?" Johnson asked Aikman. "Did I tell you the difference in the game would be turnovers? It got to be a feeding frenzy!" he said as he stepped off the escalator and strode toward the ballroom and the assembled media. "I mean, puh-leeze!"

Just remember, for the Dallas Cowboys it's only the beginning.   ★

POSTSCRIPT *The dynasty tag would fit well as the Cowboys would win two of the next three Super Bowls. In this game, Aikman, who threw four touchdown passes while completing 22 of 30 for 273 yards, was named the Super Bowl MVP (ironically, it happened in the Rose Bowl where Aikman played while in college at UCLA—but never led his team to the Rose Bowl game on New Year's Day). Outside of football circles, though, this Super Bowl may be best remembered for the extravagant 21-minute halftime performance by Michael Jackson.*

1993

A HAPPY, HUNGRY MAN

BEHOLD MICHAEL IRVIN, WITH A LUST FOR THE LAVISH AND A MOUTH THAT WON'T QUIT

BY SALLY JENKINS

AYOUNG MICHAEL IRVIN sits in the kitchen, working his way through an entire box of cornflakes. He is eating out of a large mixing bowl. He eats fast, swallowing the cereal in huge gulps. He doesn't know if he's full. He can't tell. He can't really taste the cornflakes either, because there is no milk. He is eating the cereal with tap water. All he knows is that he's going to eat it before somebody else does. The others will be home soon.

When his brothers and sisters discover that he has eaten their next day's breakfast they will beat him up, but the fear of a whipping is nothing compared with the gnawing want. There are 17 Irvin children, of which Michael is the 15th. They live in a poor Fort Lauderdale neighborhood, in a small brick house with only one fan for all the children. They fight over food, beds and cool air.

Michael Irvin is 27 now, but his ravenous appetite has not been appeased. It has only become more expensive, graduating from cornflakes with tap water to clams casino with white wine. "I crave things," he says. His urge to eat anything that doesn't blink is accompanied by a compulsion to say anything he thinks and buy anything that shines.

It's your average weekday, and Irvin is arrayed in burgundy shorts, a paisley silk shirt, gold and diamond rings on his fingers, a large diamond stud in his left ear, a diamond bracelet on one wrist, a diamond-encrusted Rolex on the other and a necklace culminating in a diamond-laden triangle the size of an ashtray. Irvin steps into a black Mercedes convertible with windows untinted so everybody can see him. "Top down, top down!" he hollers as he turns the ignition key and retracts the top, an arrogant gesture not unlike the one he makes when he removes his Dallas Cowboy helmet so that all may view him.

Irvin is the NFL's grand master of braggadocio, and he has backed up his boasts. Now in his sixth NFL season, he has helped transform the Cowboys from a 1–15 team into defending Super Bowl champions. The Mercedes was a gift to himself for signing a three-year, $3.75 million contract in 1992. The necklace was the reward Irvin gave to Irvin for his game-breaking Super Bowl performance against the Buffalo Bills, including two touchdowns in 15 seconds. He comes from the slightly-larger-than-life school of athletic celebrity. "Everybody says, 'Look at that hot dog, that cocky so-and-so,'" he says. "I'm just having fun. I'm a bad example because I enjoy myself? They take me all wrong."

The truth is, Irvin is a complicated man with a quick intelligence and formidable charm. But he is not a man of moderation. What will ever be enough for him? He has his looks, his health and as much talent as any wide receiver in the NFL. He has a Super Bowl ring to go with the national championship ring he won with the Miami Hurricanes in 1987. He has a beautiful wife, Sandy, who is a former Miami Dolphins cheerleader, and he has his own TV show in Dallas. Game over. Right? "I'm still hungry," he says. ★

POSTSCRIPT *Irvin's appetite would eventually extend to illicit fare; in March 1996 he was arrested for cocaine possession, pled no contest, was sentenced to community service plus four years probation and was suspended by the NFL for five games. There would follow two more drug-related arrests but no convictions. Despite those sins, he landed in the Cowboys Ring of Honor and the Pro Football Hall of Fame, and became a successful— and still uninhibited—TV broadcaster.*

★ *Irvin has never shown restraint when touting his skills or showing himself off, but his childhood past helps to explain why.*

Excerpted from SPORTS ILLUSTRATED *October 25, 1993*

1994

CURE FOR A HEADACHE

A PAIR OF KEY TURNOVERS HELPED THE COWBOYS AND THEIR GROGGY QUARTERBACK BEAT THE BILLS

BY PAUL ZIMMERMAN

SUPER BOWL XXVIII WILL go down in history as a blowout, because that's what a 30–13 score will look like when you read it in the record book. But the score won't come close to telling the story. The Buffalo Bills, short-enders for the fourth straight year, had the Dallas Cowboys on the ropes at the Georgia Dome in Atlanta, and they let them escape.

The story of this strange Super Bowl began a week earlier in a darkened room at Baylor University Medical Center in Dallas, where Troy Aikman lay in an eerie, semiconscious twilight. He had been knocked unconscious by the right knee of San Francisco 49er defensive end Dennis Brown in the third quarter of the Cowboys' 38–21 win that afternoon in the NFC title game. "It was scary," says Aikman's agent, Leigh Steinberg. "We sat there, he and I, alone in the dark, and his head was kind of in a cloud. He kept asking me the same questions over and over."

By 4 a.m. Aikman was beginning to function. Seventeen hours later he was standing at a podium at a press conference in the Cowboys' hotel in Atlanta, answering questions about things he had trouble remembering. Yes, Aikman confirmed, on the sideline he had turned to injured center Mark Stepnoski, on crutches and in civvies, and asked him why he wasn't playing. No, Aikman said, he didn't have a headache. "I'll be fine," he said.

Fine? Not exactly. After Dallas's Wednesday practice, Aikman was troubled by headaches. In boxing, when a fighter takes a 10 count, he is not permitted to get back into the ring for as long as 90 days in some states. In football it's called "getting your bell rung," and a week later the guy is back in uniform—if the game is big enough. On Super Sunday there was Aikman, lining up under center for the first Cowboy snap. But he was just a tiny bit off on his reads and on his deliveries, especially the short stuff. A four-yard dump-off to tight end Jay Novacek in the first quarter was low, and Novacek had to make a twisting effort to get to the ball. Two plays later his throw to Kevin Williams on a little crossing pattern underneath the zone was wide and incomplete. Aikman's completion percentage for the afternoon, 19 of 27, was good—hey, the guy could complete 70% in his sleep—but his timing was off, even on the completions.

"Off? What do you mean, off?" Novacek said later, bristling. "We won the damn game, didn't we? What kind of stupid question is that? Troy was Troy."

Of course, the Cowboys did not have to rely on Aikman's arm alone. James Washington, a reserve safety, turned the game around with two terrific second-half plays, a 46-yard fumble return for a touchdown early in the third quarter to tie the score at 13–13, and an interception at the beginning of the fourth quarter to set up the score that put the game away. And Emmitt Smith, on the strength of his 30 carries for 132 yards and two touchdowns, was named the MVP.

A lot of the postgame buzz in the Dallas locker room was, naturally, about a dynasty. As the last of the Cowboys trickled out, Nate Newton paused for one final salvo at the journalists who had hounded the Dallas players all week. "Goodbye, media," shouted the voluble lineman. "All the others hate you. I love you. I embrace you. Bye, now." You almost expected him to add, "See you again next year." ★

POSTSCRIPT *The Cowboys would return to the Super Bowl—not the next year but the year after. As for Aikman's head, when he retired after the 2000 season—and the 10th concussion of his career—he indicated it was "because of my health, the concussions, the back problems. It took its toll."*

★ *The game turned on a fumble by Buffalo's Thurman Thomas (34) that was returned for a TD by the Cowboys' Washington.*

Excerpted from SPORTS ILLUSTRATED *February 7, 1994*

1994

THE UNLIKELY COWBOY

JERRY JONES PARTED WITH JIMMY JOHNSON THEN DOUBLED THE SHOCK WHEN HE HIRED BARRY SWITZER

BY RICK TELANDER

SOMEBODY SAY WISHBONE? "Yep," says Barry Switzer, the Oklahoma Sooners'—excuse us— the new Dallas Cowboys' coach. "Figured we'd line up in the wishbone for the first play of the season. Troy down the line, pitch to Emmitt, me right behind. Emmitt running all the way and me yelling, 'I knew it would work! I knew it would work!'"

You want to clear your throat here, check Switzer's eyes. Because stranger things have happened. "Uh-huh, I heard that," says Emmitt Smith, the all-world running back. "He was joking." Smith pauses to make sure he's been understood. "He was joking."

O.K., O.K. It's just, how do we know with these Cowboys? If owner Jerry Jones said he was moving the Cowboys to Brazil tomorrow and naming Pelé the defensive coordinator, would you doubt him? Jones is the guy who won the last two Super Bowls, and then, in March, suddenly let Jimmy Johnson go and hired former Oklahoma coach and social outcast Switzer.

To appreciate Switzer's lack of appeal to the football community—and thus the audacity of Jones's decision—consider that Switzer had been sitting in a rocking chair in Norman, Okla., for five years with an imaginary sign around his neck saying WOULDN'T MIND COACHING AGAIN, and that until Jones beckoned, tumbleweed made more noise than Switzer's phone. "I think I found out Jerry wanted me by hearing it on TV," says Switzer.

Quarterback Troy Aikman was not thrilled when Johnson left. What Aikman feels now more than anything is a kind of vertigo caused by the linked, circular paths of the principals of this soap opera. To wit: Jones was a teammate of Johnson's at Arkansas,

where one of the assistants was Switzer, who had earlier played for the Razorbacks. Johnson and Switzer were assistants together at Oklahoma, before Switzer became the head man there and Johnson became the coach at archrival Oklahoma State. Aikman gave a verbal commitment to attend Oklahoma State after Johnson recruited him, but then Aikman visited Oklahoma and believed Switzer's promise that the Sooners would change their option attack to the I formation, just for Aikman. So Aikman enrolled at Oklahoma. Switzer didn't change the attack; Aikman broke his leg as a sophomore against Johnson's new team, Miami, and promptly transferred to UCLA in a move facilitated by Switzer. As a Cowboy under Johnson, Aikman became a Pro Bowl quarterback and never dreamed he would play once more for the man who had lured him to Norman a decade ago and then helped him depart for Los Angeles.

Cowboy publicist Rich Dalrymple is an easygoing chap who worked for Johnson at Miami before joining the Dallas front office in 1990. Some people have said that if Dalrymple, a skillful peacemaker, had been at the table in Orlando on that night four months ago when Jones and Johnson had the climactic clash that led to Johnson's departure, Johnson would still be the Dallas coach. But Dalrymple had left the table when Jones arrived to offer a toast, only to be snubbed by Johnson and friends. Says Dalrymple now, "I asked myself how the coverage and hype could increase after our last championship. I figured the only way was if we won a third straight Super Bowl. I was wrong." ★

POSTSCRIPT *In Switzer's first season, the Cowboys would finish 12–4 but lose in the NFC title game to the 49ers. In his second season, to the surprise of many doubters, he led Dallas back to another Super Bowl victory. After a 6–10 season in 1997, he resigned.*

★ *Switzer's arrival in Dallas was met with more than a little skepticism, but the affable coach thought he'd fit in comfortably.*

Excerpted from SPORTS ILLUSTRATED *August 1, 1994*

1996

PRINCE OF THE CITY

THE BELOVED COWBOYS QUARTERBACK HAD IT ALL—EXCEPT FOR A STEADY GIRLFRIEND

BY JOHN ED BRADLEY

TROY AIKMAN, WHO TURNED 29 IN November, might be the most eligible bachelor to play in the NFL since Joe Willie Namath hung up his white cleats. But while this is an image for which many single men would sell their mortal souls, it isn't one Aikman much appreciates. He would rather have a wife and four kids. ★ "I really thought I'd be married by now," he says. I was 22 my rookie year. If you had asked me then how old I'd be when I got married, I'd have said, 'Oh, 26, 27.' Well, here I am not even seriously involved with anybody." ★ It's his own fault, of course. "Troy," says his best friend on the team, guard-center Dale Hellestrae, "has more opportunities with women than any man on this earth. But he's got his particular tastes, and he's not going to settle for anything below his sight level. He won't compromise. I've never tried to set

Excerpted from
SPORTS ILLUSTRATED
January 15, 1996

★ *Though he was just an Oklahoma country boy at heart, it was fair to say that Aikman owned this town.*

him up, because I don't think I could find anyone who'd meet his qualifications."

Aikman has every right to hold out for just the right gal. To start, he's rich beyond practical measure. Two years ago he signed an eight-year, $50 million contract that made him the highest-paid player in pro football history. He's also tall, blond and blue-eyed: the kind of dreamboat who used to star in horse and tank pictures. He is, moreover, the leader of the most valuable franchise in all of sports.

No player in the league means more to his team than Aikman does. Dallas isn't Dallas when he isn't on the field, and nobody is more aware of this than the Cowboys players themselves.

During a recent practice drill, Aikman fired off one perfect pass after another, his delivery quick and sharp. Unable to contain himself any longer, loquacious wide receiver Michael Irvin beat his hands together and shouted in something of a singsong voice, "I love you, 'Roy." It was spontaneous and beautiful, and everyone laughed, but Irvin meant it. "I attribute my success to him," Irvin says later. "The greatest things, the greatest times—Troy is 100% responsible, and even then I'm understating it."

And yet, despite his kinship with Aikman, Irvin rarely ribs him about his status as the game's latest, greatest heartthrob. This is a situation that requires sensitivity. One day *Cosmopolitan* magazine calls to quiz Aikman about his love life, the next a national newspaper does the same. Aikman entertains the queries with a mixture of curiosity and exasperation, wondering how his image ever came to this.

"In the last few years Troy's become so big, he's almost like a prisoner," says former Cowboys quarterback Babe Laufenberg, a close friend. "People get weird when they see him. And every time you go out with him something totally unexpected happens. Every time. As a result, he can't do much anymore. 'Where do you want to go?' you ask him. 'I don't know,' he says. 'Pick a place.' 'O.K., [here].' 'That place is going to be so crowded, it's not going to be any fun. Too many people. I'll just get hassled.' 'Fine. What about [here]?' 'Oh, no. There's nothing going on there.' So you end up going back to his house and watching TV. That's your big night out with Troy."

AIKMAN'S BACKGROUND DOESN'T SUGGEST that he was fated for such peculiar problems. Although he spent his early childhood in Southern California, his formative years belong to Henryetta, Okla., a town of

about 6,500 people. Troy was 12 when his family moved to a 172-acre parcel of land near Henryetta to fulfill his father's dream of operating a ranch. In California, Troy had dreamed of playing pro baseball. He had practiced signing his autograph, imagining lines of fans desperate to get it. But all that stopped when he got to Henryetta.

 THEIR FRIEND-ship got a boost when Aikman bought a tropical fish tank. A couple of times Johnson called him and said, "Mind if I stop by and check out your tank?"

"We ended up seven miles out of town on dirt roads that were too rough to ride your bike on," he says. "It was tough. Even at that age I could see my athletic career falling apart."

Before school in the mornings Troy fed slop to the pigs. In the summer he hauled hay in the fields, often late into the night. His best class was typing, and there he had no peer. One year he won a typing contest at a place called Okmulgee State Tech, producing 75 words a minute. He was a good player on a mediocre football team—the Henryetta Fighting Hens.

Nonetheless, Troy was eager for fame to find him. By the time he was a junior, folks in Oklahoma recognized his name as belonging to the tall string bean of a kid with the amazing right arm. In 1984 Oklahoma University invited Troy to a summer football camp. "I remember an assistant comes to me and says he has this quarterback he wants me to meet," recalls Barry Switzer, then the OU coach and now the head coach of the Cowboys. "I asked him, 'Is he black?' He answered, 'No, Barry, he's white. But he's got 4.6 speed, and he's got an arm.' I remember the first time I ever saw Troy. I walked out on the practice field and somebody threw him a football, and I stopped and watched him. He threw the ball back, and I said to myself, This kid is different. I watched him throw it five or six times, and then I said it again, Yeah, he's different. I offered him a scholarship

on the spot, which I don't remember ever having done before with a quarterback. But then I'd never seen a kid who could throw the ball like he could."

"I'd been in Dallas a year when Troy got here," Irvin says. "I remember the first day he showed up. We were throwing and catching, and he had this zip on the ball. And his ball was easy to catch. It had all the speed in the world, and it would come to you and hover. It would actually hover. The ball seemed to be saying, 'O.K., Michael, you can catch me now.' I've never seen anybody throw a better ball."

He went 0–11 as a rookie, the lowest-rated quarterback in the league. He missed five games with a broken finger, and when he came back he suffered a concussion—the first of several in his NFL career, after two in college. Eighteen months into his pro career Aikman finally won a game, one of seven the Cowboys would win in 1990. The next year they won 11 before losing to Detroit in the playoffs. Then they went 13–3 in 1992 and beat the Buffalo Bills by 35 points in Super Bowl XXVII. Aikman threw for 273 yards and four touchdowns and was named MVP. Before the night was over Aikman would find himself cast as the most celebrated athlete in the world—"America's quarterback," as Irvin likes to call him.

Aikman went on the morning shows of the three

★ *With Aikmania rampant, Troy could rarely be alone in public. Said a friend, "He's so big he's almost like a prisoner."*

major networks. And then he made his first appearance on *The Tonight Show*. Meanwhile, back in Texas, something called "Aikmania" was in full, glorious bloom. The *Dallas Morning News* ran a story called "A Fan's Guide to Troy," which noted, "All single women in America may join together in a collective sigh of relief. His Troyness is still available."

With the shared experience of consecutive Super Bowl wins, he and Jimmy Johnson sought each other out on a more personal level. Their friendship got a real boost when Aikman bought a tropical fish tank. Fish were one of Johnson's great passions. "When I told Jimmy about my tank he got really fired up," Aikman says. "He came over and set up my rocks, my reefs and everything—he did all of it."

"I enjoyed the fish," Johnson says, "but it wasn't only that. I saw this as an opportunity to get to know Troy better." A couple of times Johnson called Aikman and said, "Mind if I stop by and check out your tank?"

"Heck, no," Aikman said. "Come on over." Johnson usually arrived with an ice chest full of beer and a thousand stories to tell. "We'd sit there," Aikman says, "and drink some beer and talk about the fish and whatever. Jimmy was so relaxed, you could tell that this was what made him happy."

Later Aikman flew down to the Bahamas for a vacation and Johnson joined him for a night in the casino. Johnson left in the morning for Orlando and the annual NFL owners' meeting, where he would have a tense barroom encounter with Jones. "That was the last time I saw Jimmy as head coach of this football team," Aikman says. In the days that followed Johnson stepped down as coach, and Jones replaced him with Switzer.

"Troy carries more pressure now with Jimmy being gone," Laufenberg says. "Jimmy was such a dominating and domineering figure. Barry's style is real laissez-faire. He sees it as the players' team.'"

"Yeah, but you know what?" says Irvin. "What Troy is doing now is what he's done all the time. It's just being noticed more because Jimmy's not here. People say, 'Well, who's leading the team?' It's the same people who've always led the team. It's Troy. Troy leads this team." ★

POSTSCRIPT *On April 8, 2000, Aikman would marry Rhonda Worthey, a former Cowboys publicist, with whom he would raise three daughters. The 2000 season would be his last. In 2006 he was inducted into the Pro Football Hall of Fame. Both Aikman and Johnson would become successful network broadcasters covering NFL games, Aikman being nominated three times for an Emmy Award.*

1996

BARRY'S HAPPY ENDING

AFTER A SEASON DODGING CRITICS, BARRY SWITZER GOT THE LAST LAUGH AS HIS COWBOYS WON THE TITLE

BY MICHAEL SILVER

THERE WAS ENOUGH LOVE, booze and R-rated language to fill a Texas-sized swimming pool Sunday night in Barry Switzer's hotel suite when the coach of the Super Bowl–champion Dallas Cowboys finally got his deliverance. It came in the form of a hug and a speech from a man wearing a checkered suit, black derby hat and superfluous sunglasses. Several hours after the Cowboys had defeated the Pittsburgh Steelers 27–17 in Super Bowl XXX at Sun Devil Stadium in Tempe, Ariz., flamboyant Dallas receiver Michael Irvin burst into suite 4000 at The Buttes resort and offered a tribute that brought Switzer to tears. "Hey, let me ask you something," Irvin shouted to the assembled revelers. "Is there anyone who deserves this more than Barry Switzer?"

"Hell, no!" answered 50 or 60 of Switzer's closest friends and family members. After Irvin had finished his speech, the gang went back to singing Switzer's praises, offering pronouncements of unbridled affection for a man who, despite his team's Super Bowl triumph, will probably be remembered as the most maligned coach ever to have won an NFL championship.

Had the heavily favored Cowboys lost this game, something that seemed quite possible late in the fourth quarter, the defeat would have finally provided critics with enough ammunition to demolish Switzer. Yet by Sunday night Switzer was a Super Bowl champion. Bash him all you like, but give the 58-year-old coach his due. The same goes for owner Jerry Jones and the rest of the Cowboys, who, in becoming only the second team to win five Super Bowls (the San Francisco 49ers share the distinction) and the first to win three Super Bowls in a four-year span, traveled an exceedingly bumpy road.

"Our guys have taken a lot of shots. Our character has been questioned," Dallas defensive end Tony Tolbert said after the game. "But we came through, and now it's time for us to do the celebrating we deserve."

For better or worse, Switzer was vindicated on a temperate evening in the Valley of the Sun. The Cowboys scored on their first three possessions and took a 13–0 lead six minutes before halftime. The Steelers survived by gutting out a 13-play, 54-yard drive that ended with quarterback Neil O'Donnell throwing a six-yard touchdown pass to wideout Yancey Thigpen 13 seconds before the intermission.

A game was on, and had it not been for Larry Brown's two second-half interceptions—on O'Donnell passes that seemed as though they were intended for the Dallas cornerback (who was named the game's MVP)—it might well have been the Steelers heading off into the night in search of a victory party. Both interceptions set up Cowboys touchdowns, the latter a four-yard run by tailback Emmitt Smith that clinched the game with 3:43 to go.

Back in the suite on Sunday night, the broadest grin belonged to Switzer as he sipped Jack Daniel's and prepared for what would likely be the sweetest hangover of his life. "This is all you need to know about life," he said. "Compassion and love and caring will take you the furthest. You've got to be around for 50 or 60 or 70 years, so you might as well do it that way."

Mark it down in history: For the 1995 season, and for Super Bowl XXX, Barry's way was the right way. ★

POSTSCRIPT *Switzer lasted two more seasons with the Cowboys. Then began a decade of instability and a parade of head coaches: Chan Gailey, Dave Campo, Bill Parcells and Wade Phillips. None of them was able to return the Cowboys to the Super Bowl.*

★ *Switzer enjoyed the chill of victory as Leon Lett (78) and Super Bowl MVP Brown (24) did the icy honors.*

Excerpted from SPORTS ILLUSTRATED *February 5, 1996*

1996

WHAT'S THE RUSH?

DON'T BE FOOLED BY THAT POSE. EMMITT SMITH'S IMPROBABLE MISSION REVEALED A DRIVEN MAN

BY JOHN ED BRADLEY

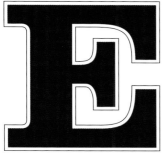

EMMITT SMITH WAS home alone one night in April, minding his own business, when the old picture started crowding his head again. It was Walter Payton, the former Chicago Bears great who rushed for more yards than any back in NFL history. Payton was wearing his familiar number 34. He had that big C on the side of his helmet, and he was chomping on that funny-looking mouthpiece. And he was running, running because that's how Emmitt sees him whenever the picture comes back: Payton slipping past the defense, Payton finding open field, Payton scoring a touchdown.

This night a torrent of numbers came trailing after the picture, and Emmitt felt compelled to write them down. He got out a pen and a piece of paper and made a note that Payton had rushed for almost 17,000 yards in his career. Next to that figure Emmitt scribbled the number 9,000, which is approximately how many yards he had gained since joining the Dallas Cowboys in 1990.

On the page the difference seemed incredible. Payton's figure looked huge, almost epic, while Emmitt's seemed small and insignificant. After considering the disparity for a while, Emmitt did some simple arithmetic. *If over the next five years you gain 1,500 yards a season*, he said to himself, *that'll give you another 7,500.*

He was writing furiously now, his face crimped with intensity. It was history, after all, that he was trying to draw a bead on: a place where no runner had ever gone before. *Add the 7,500 to the 9,000 you've already gained*, he continued, *and your total is 16,500.*

It was still a few hundred yards short of Payton's mark. But there was something else to consider. In five years Emmitt would be 31. Payton finished his playing career at 33.

"I can be there," Emmitt said later, fixating again on the great Walter Payton. "But I've got to hit one helluva pace. I've got to get ahead of the curve … and I can do that. There's time, there's time."

Back when Emmitt was a student at Escambia High in Pensacola, Fla., his football coach used to say, "It's a dream until you write it down. Then it's a goal." And Emmitt never forgot that. He all but branded the words on his heart, and he was always writing things down. When Emmitt was a rookie, before he had even played his first game, one of his Dallas teammates, safety James Washington, stopped by to visit him at his apartment and found Emmitt sitting and writing things like "rookie of the year" and "leading rusher" on a piece of paper.

"What are you doing?" Washington asked.

Emmitt held up the list. "This is what I want to accomplish this season."

Emmitt is no different when it comes to business. Write it down and it isn't a dream—it's a goal. "Not long ago," says Everett Brooks, marketing manager for Emmitt Smith Communications, one of four business enterprises Emmitt presides over, "Emmitt came in and sat down and started putting together an organization chart detailing exactly where he wants to be in six months. He knows what he wants. And nothing will stop him." ★

POSTSCRIPT *Six years later on Oct. 27, 2002, at Texas Stadium, Smith, at the age of 33—almost precisely as he had written it down—took a handoff and ran off left tackle on a play called 15 Lead, gaining 11 yards against the Seattle Seahawks, thereby breaking Walter Payton's rushing record. He would retire with 18,355 yards, the NFL's alltime rushing leader.*

★ *Smith seemed content to relax in his new pool. But not for long—there were businesses to run and records to run down.*

Excerpted from SPORTS ILLUSTRATED *July 1, 1996*

THE 1990s TEXAS STYLE

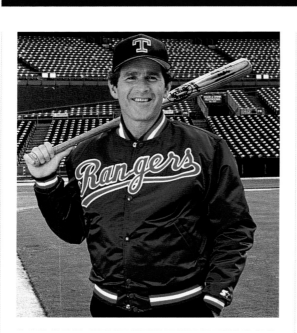

★ In '92 George W. Bush was part-owner of the Rangers, in '94 the governor of Texas, in '99 a candidate for President.

★ On Walker, Texas Ranger, *Chuck Norris staked his claim as top TV cowboy.*

★ Ann Richards lost the Texas governorship to Bush in '94; though a hunter, she voted to curtail firearms.

★ *In '91 the* Times Herald *shut down, with the Cowboys atop the final front page; in '97,* D Magazine *probed the Cowboys' misadventures.*

★ *Presidential candidate Ross Perot, Dallas billionaire, took aim at Bill Clinton's record.*

In *Walker, Texas Ranger,* Walker's partner was Jimmy Trivette (played by Clarence Gilyard). The character was a former Cowboys football player. (Gilyard was not.)

★ *The Stars moved to Dallas from Minnesota in '93; five seasons later Mike Modano led them to the Stanley Cup.*

★ *When Michael Irvin showed up at court on drug possession charges, his garb included a full-length mink.*

★ *LaDainian Tomlinson put TCU back on the football map with his heroics.*

THE 1990s IN PICTURES

★ *Never known as a runner, Troy Aikman took off against the Bills in Super Bowl XXVII; his four touchdown passes earned him MVP.*
★ *Called "Moose" by all, fullback Daryl Johnston was a bull with the ball but earned more kudos as a blocking back for Emmitt Smith.*

★ *Bill Bates (40), an undersized overachiever, made himself a fan favorite (and an All-Pro) as an all-out, hell-bent special teams player.*
★ *"Neon" Deion Sanders had his flamboyant tag before joining the Cowboys in '95, but in Dallas he secured his rep as a lockdown corner.*

★ *In the Cowboys last championship season,'95, Emmitt Smith led the way with 1,773 yards rushing and 25 TDs, both career bests.*

★ *Mark Stepnoski, a five-time Pro Bowler, centered the great '90s lines of talented giants named Newton, Williams and Tuinei.*

★ *At Super Bowl XXVII, the Dallas Cowboys Cheerleaders made their own claim to best in the business with their moment in the sun.*
★ *The Big Three were all first-round draft picks in successive years: Irvin in '88 (#11 overall), Aikman in '89 (#1), Smith in '90 (#17).*

★ Sturdy, consistent and dominating, Michael Irvin (here in Green Bay in '97) led Dallas in receiving eight straight seasons, '91 through '98.
★ Thomas Everett's interception halted a Buffalo drive in SB XXVII, as LBs Ken Norton Jr. (51) and Robert Jones (55) admired the grab.

★ *In Super Bowl XXX, DB Deion Sanders took a turn as a receiver, helping the Cowboys to a convincing 27–17 victory over the Steelers.*
★ *Jay Novacek, one in a string of brilliant Cowboys tight ends (Dupree-Cosbie-Novacek-Witten), starred in Dallas from '90 through '95.*

★ *Darren Woodson, a force at strong safety for twelve seasons, made off with an interception in a Jan. '94 playoff win over Green Bay.*
★ *Another gem of the Dallas scouting system, Pro Bowler Leon Lett was drafted in the seventh round in '91 out of Emporia State.*

★ *Defenders strewn in his wake, Emmitt Smith scored as Dallas
knocked off the Niners 30–20 for the NFC title in Jan. '93.*

★ *WR Alvin Harper added some icing after his 45-yard TD catch
in Super Bowl XXVII, much to the delight of Michael Irvin.*

1990S: THE ROUNDUP

★ ALL-DECADE TEAM ★

OFFENSE

QB ★ TROY AIKMAN (1989–2000)

RB ★ EMMITT SMITH (1990–2002)

FB ★ DARYL JOHNSTON (1989–99)

WR ★ MICHAEL IRVIN (1988–99)

WR ★ ALVIN HARPER (1991–94, '99)

TE ★ JAY NOVACEK (1990–96)

T ★ MARK TUINEI (1983–97)

G ★ NATE NEWTON (1986–98)

C ★ MARK STEPNOSKI (1989–94, 1999–2001)

G ★ LARRY ALLEN (1994–2005)

T ★ ERIK WILLIAMS (1991–2000)

K ★ CHRIS BONIOL (1994–96)

RET ★ KEVIN WILLIAMS (1993–96)

DEFENSE

DE ★ CHARLES HALEY (1992–96)

DT ★ RUSSELL MARYLAND (1991–95)

DT ★ TONY CASILLAS (1991–93, '96–97)

DE ★ TONY TOLBERT (1989–97)

LB ★ RANDALL GODFREY (1996–99)

LB ★ KEN NORTON (1988–93)

LB ★ ROBERT JONES (1992–95)

DB ★ DARREN WOODSON (1992–2003)

DB ★ LARRY BROWN (1991–95, '98)

DB ★ KEVIN SMITH (1992–99)

DB ★ DEION SANDERS (1995–99)

P ★ JOHN JETT (1993–96)

COACH ★ JIMMY JOHNSON (1989–93)

BEST DRAFT SURPRISE

LARRY BROWN CB TCU ▶
Drafted 12th round, 1991, 320th overall

The late pick of the little-known cornerback (the 56th DB selected) punctuated one of the finest drafts ever (nine starters in 18 selections, including Russell Maryland, Alvin Harper, Erik Williams and Leon Lett). Brown started in his first five seasons in Dallas and, with two interceptions of Neil O'Donnell, was MVP of Super Bowl XXX.

BIGGEST DRAFT BUST

SHANE HANNAH OG MICHIGAN STATE
Drafted 2nd round, 1995, 63rd overall

After missing his rookie season with a torn right knee ligament, Hannah returned for training camp in 1996 overweight and undermotivated. He was cut in the '96 preseason and tried a comeback the following year only to be waived again. He never played in an NFL game but left Dallas with a '95 Super Bowl ring.

★ A COWBOY TO REMEMBER *In his short time in Dallas, linebacker Randall Godfrey had a big impact—a team-leading 242 tackles in four Cowboy seasons.*

★ Training table: Nate Newton, weighing in at around 320 pounds, had little use for proper diet, letting the chips fall where they might.

> BY THE NUMBERS

117 Consecutive games from 1990 to '98 in which Michael Irvin had at least one reception, a Cowboys record.

71 Times the Cowboys have appeared on *Monday Night Football* (through 2009), including 23 times in the 1990s. Only the Miami Dolphins (73) have been seen more on Monday nights.

45 Weeks in a row that the Cowboys were *not* seen on *Monday Night Football*, starting after Week 5 of 1988 and ending in Week 2 of 1991.

90 Yard pass from Troy Aikman to Alvin Harper against the 49ers on Nov. 13, 1994, on which Harper did not score. It's the third longest non-touchdown pass in the NFL since the 1970 merger.

43 Million dollars in contracts Jerry Jones signed in 1995 with Pepsi and Nike to be the official brands of Texas Stadium, thus unilaterally defying the NFL's licensing agreements with Coca-Cola and three apparel companies.

5 Super Bowl rings for defensive end Charles Haley, an NFL record. Haley joined the Cowboys in 1992 having won two titles with the 49ers. In Dallas, he was an integral part of three more.

WILLIAM PRINCE DAVIS, SEPTEMBER 14, 1999
Convicted murderer, just before his execution in Huntsville, Texas:

"I'd like to say in closing, What about those Cowboys!"

OVERLOOKED GAME OF THE DECADE

SEPTEMBER 7, 1992 VS. REDSKINS In the season opener, the Redskins came to Dallas as reigning Super Bowl champs. The Cowboys were considered, at best, a work in progress. On a sweaty 86° Monday evening, Dallas scored on offense (an Emmitt Smith run, an Alvin Harper catch), defense (an Issiac Holt sack in the end zone for a safety) and with the return game (a 79-yard punt return by Kelvin Martin) for a convincing 23–10 win. And so began the Cowboys run to their first Super Bowl title in 15 years.

WHAT WERE THEY THINKING?

MARCH 29, 1994 Together Jerry Jones and Jimmy Johnson had, in five years, transformed the Cowboys from the NFL's worst team into its two-time champion. But the two old college teammates, with egos of matching size, decided they couldn't coexist. Even Barry Switzer, the handpicked replacement for Johnson, couldn't fathom it, asking Jones: "Would you or Jimmy please explain to me how two guys could be on top of the world and win two straight Super Bowls and not be able to get along with each other?"

★ IT'S A FACT: *Former University of Miami coach Jimmy Johnson went with what he knew—he brought 10 Hurricanes to Dallas in his five seasons.*

The ⭐20

★ ADAMS ★   ★ ALLEN ★   ★ JONES ★   ★ PARCELLS ★   ★ WITTEN ★

A difficult decade ended, followed quickly by a

00's

★ NEWMAN ★   ★ ROMO ★   ★ WARE ★   ★ AUSTIN ★   ★ DAVIS ★

playoff win and the promise of more to come

★ *Among the amenities at the new Cowboys Stadium, opened in 2009, are the enormous video screens—which proved a tempting target to punters.*

GREG NELSON

2006

A SUDDEN STAR

QUARTERBACK TONY ROMO CAME OUT OF NOWHERE TO REVIVE THE COWBOYS

BY TIM LAYDEN

EVERYTHING TURNED ON JUST three words. An old quarterback was cast aside, and a young quarterback was offered his place. A fabled franchise was reinvigorated and its silver-haired future Hall of Fame coach was transformed from listless and sad to vibrant and feisty. Talk of rebuilding morphed suddenly into talk of winning the Super Bowl. Three words. "Romo, you're in!" shouted Dallas Cowboys quarterbacks coach Chris Palmer on the night of Monday, Oct. 23, in the team's Texas Stadium locker room at halftime of the Cowboys' game against the New York Giants. ★ "Not very romantic, I guess," says Tony Romo of Palmer's order to replace starter Drew Bledsoe, delivered on behalf of coach Bill Parcells, only when the Cowboys had reached the brink of desperation, and worse, absurdity. They trailed the Giants 12–7. A loss would drop them to 3–3, and soon thereafter the Cowboys' 2006 season would be remembered as the year in which Terrell Owens did or did not try to kill

Excerpted from
SPORTS ILLUSTRATED
December 11, 2006

★ *Largely unrecruited for college and undrafted by the NFL, Romo's rise said as much about will as skill.*

DAVID BERGMAN

himself and Parcells ended his coaching career with a whimper, a beaten bit player in an embarrassing dark comedy.

Romo, 26, had not taken a meaningful snap since the Cowboys signed him as an undrafted free agent from Division I-AA Eastern Illinois in 2003 and buried him on the depth chart, behind the likes of Quincy Carter, Chad Hutchinson and Clint Stoerner. And he did not lead the Cowboys to a comeback win over the Giants that night. He threw three second-half interceptions in a 36–22 loss.

Since that defeat, however, the Cowboys have won five of six games, including Sunday's 23–20 victory over the Giants in New Jersey. Romo's production has been stunning: He has completed 67.8% of his passes and leads the NFL with a 102.4 passer rating. The Giants hammered Romo with blitzes, yet at the end of an often frustrating afternoon (20 for 34, 257 yards, no touchdowns, two interceptions and a fumble), Romo and the Cowboys were still in position to win.

With six seconds left in the game, Dallas lined up for a potential game-winning 46-yard field goal by their new kicker, Martin Gramatica. The Giants called timeout to unnerve the emotional Gramatica, who was signed only five days earlier. When the play clock was started, Romo, the holder, walked up behind his offensive linemen and shouted at them to keep their heads. "I told them not to move if the Giants start calling fake timeouts," Romo said. "Because you can't call two in a row, but they might try to get us to false start, and we didn't need to lose five more yards."

Gramatica nailed the kick. Romo's legend grew. "This kid is for real," says Cowboys veteran guard Marco Rivera. "He can take charge in the huddle. He can lead the team. He can play."

 HE THIRD CHILD, AND first son, born to Ramiro and Joan (née Jakubowski) Romo came into the world in 1980, while Ramiro was stationed at a U.S. naval base in San Diego. "My family is from Mexico," says Ramiro. "Tony's mom's family is part Polish, part German. Tony is Heinz 57."

Romo, the best athlete in Burlington, Wis.—became the starting quarterback as a junior at Burlington High and threw for 308 yards in his first start. A year later the team went 3–6; Romo got few calls from recruiters. "You know those guys who threw a nice,

tight spiral in high school?" says Romo. "That wasn't me." In truth, he was better at basketball (a 24-point average as a senior), but as a 6'2" scoring guard he surmised that he had more upside in football and accepted a partial scholarship to Division I-AA Eastern Illinois in Charleston, Ill., four hours from home.

Romo ascended to the starting quarterback job at Eastern as a sophomore. In three seasons he had 85 touchdown passes and 8,212 passing yards. He won the Walter Payton Award, the I-AA Heisman, as a senior, yet went undrafted. Cowboys assistant Sean Payton (a former Eastern Illinois QB himself) called Romo after the draft about signing as a free agent. He put Parcells and team owner Jerry Jones on the phone. Romo had other offers but signed with Dallas.

 ROMO ATTENDED a Mavericks game, where the crowd of 20,000 chanted his name. Says Romo, "That was the first time I felt like it was really getting different."

Bill Parcells does not so much coach quarterbacks as tolerate them. A still-developing Romo was the next in line. In his first NFL appearance, a preseason game on Aug. 9, 2003, at Arizona, Romo tried an improvised shuffle pass in the red zone, and it was intercepted. Parcells met him halfway between the huddle and sideline. "Hey, Pancho Villa!" Parcells shouted. "What was that?"

By his second season Romo's scattershot passing had earned him an upgrade to Wild Thing in Parcells's lexicon. "One day in my second year," says Romo, "I threw high over somebody because I was messing with my mechanics. Bill yells at me, 'You're too inaccurate to play in this league!' Bill doesn't want to hear excuses. You just keep working."

And now that Romo is the starter, the highest-rated quarterback in the league ... Parcells has ratcheted up the abuse.

9 TONY ROMO

67

"You're not Johnny Unitas yet, Romo!"

"You're not Joe Montana!"

Says Romo, "Ninety-five percent of it is just needling, and it's hilarious. I get along with Bill because we're both competitive. We both want the same thing."

Romo's first start came on Oct. 29, against the Panthers, six days after his relief appearance against the Giants. For five days he'd prepared for Carolina while stewing about his three-pick effort against New York. Carolina went up 14–0 in the first quarter. Tight end Jason Witten approached Romo on the sideline, where rising panic was palpable. "Listen, man, we've got to have this game," Witten told his quarterback. "You need to relax, be the leader, play within the system, because we're 3–3 and we cannot lose here."

Romo cut him off. "Jason, I've got everything under control," he said, seething. "We'll be fine." The

★ At the outset, Romo met the surge of celebrity with an air of amusement, including rumors about a certain Jessica Simpson.

Cowboys went on to win 35–14, Romo finishing 24 of 36 for 270 yards. Romo's celebrity grows daily in Dallas. The team's postseason life will last as long as he can stay grounded. On Nov. 16, three days before the Cowboys handed Indianapolis and Peyton Manning their first defeat of the season, Romo met a reporter for dinner at a modest buffet-style restaurant in a bustling North Dallas shopping-mall food court. One diner stopped by to shake Romo's hand and wish him good luck, and a woman asked to have her picture taken with him. That's it. Just two requests.

Two weeks later—after wins over the Colts and, on Thanksgiving Day, the Bucs—Romo attended a Mavericks game, where the crowd of 20,000 chanted his name. "It got a little crazy there," Romo says. "That was the first time I felt like it was really getting different."

He has handled the transformation gracefully, even when rumors were rampant in late November linking Romo to singer Jessica Simpson. He remains tight with a group of more than a dozen friends from Eastern Illinois who keep him grounded. And Romo observes his own rise with a look of bemusement. "He's not caught up in any of this," says Witten. "He just wants to win."

On Sunday evening Romo scrambled to stuff his gear into a backpack in the visitor's locker room. Less than two months ago he was a ghost who could slip away unnoticed, the second-stringer whose voice was unheard. Now his space is cluttered with visitors and media, the trappings of sudden stardom. He is the last to leave the room, moving briskly through the bowels of the stadium into the Jersey darkness, his suit jacket flapping in the night air. The team bus awaits, idling. Because now the Cowboys ride Romo.   ★

POSTSCRIPT *The ensuing ride was bumpy. The season ended abruptly on January 6, 2007, in Seattle in an NFC wild-card game. With the Cowboys down 21–20 and 1:19 left, Dallas attempted a 19-yard field goal. Romo, the holder, bobbled the snap as he tried to place the ball, then tried to run. He was tackled at the two-yard line; the Cowboys lost. The following season, on December 16, 2007 in Texas Stadium, Jessica Simpson attended a game against the Eagles; Romo played poorly in the loss and the relationship became increasingly controversial until it ended, reportedly in July 2009. With Romo as their signal-caller, the Cowboys suffered a series of season-ending miseries until 2009, when he led Dallas to its first postseason win since 1996.*

2007

THE GAMBLER STRIKES AGAIN

JERRY JONES MADE A FIRST FORTUNE IN OIL, AND A SECOND IN HIGH-STAKES FOOTBALL

BY RICHARD HOFFER

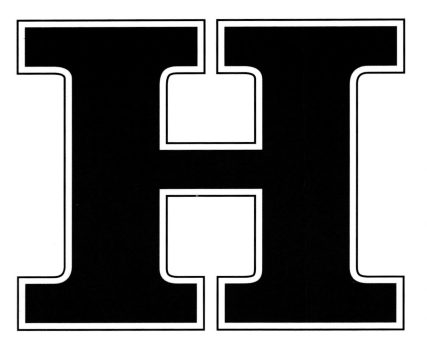

IS "TOLERANCE FOR ambiguity"—his phrase—is high enough to register somewhere between impudence and daredevilry. Where else would you put it? When the big oil companies, who are hardly in the business of prudence, abandoned their dry holes in the late '60s, it was Jerry Jones who offered to lease their failures. A dry hole, after all, is simply a gusher without conviction. Jones, then as now, supplied all the conviction necessary. ★ But let's not make him sound as if he lacked a mortal's ability to recognize consequence. When he pledged his wealth and all receivables to buy the floundering Dallas Cowboys—America's Team or not, this was a failing outfit in 1989— he needed two hands to steady a cup of coffee. Who wouldn't? In

Excerpted from
SPORTS ILLUSTRATED
July 16, 2007

★ *The massive new stadium that Jones has conjured stands as a monument to his Cowboys kingdom.*

those days Dallas was the epicenter for one of the oil industry's worst depressions. Oil, to the extent that anyone was bothering to look for it, was $10 a barrel. Titans were being wiped out, banks closed, skyscrapers shuttered. Why did the Cowboys, the one club for which Jones would revisit his childhood dream of owning an NFL team, have to come up for sale when there was blood on the streets?

Of course his hands shook. Even beyond the economic climate, the deal was punishing. It was bad enough that he had to pay $65 million for the Cowboys. The team was not very good, and after three losing seasons, home sellouts were even harder to come by than victories. Worse, Jones was forced to absorb the $75 million leasing rights on Texas Stadium. (The total price was a record for an NFL team.) In those days NFL stadiums were essentially rentals, some place you visited on Sundays. They had no income or marketing worth to NFL owners.

He had to have those Cowboys, though. On that April morning, on vacation in Cabo San Lucas, having decided to forgo a fishing trip on account of too much tequila the night before, he rattled his newspaper open to see that the Cowboys were for sale. And he knew he might be in trouble. "The Cowboys were my devil," he says.

The deal done, Jones barely had time to count the empty suites, consider the previous season's 3–13 record, and get over the surprising fact that the Cowboys had lost $9.5 million on just $41 million in revenues the year before, when the bills began to come in. They totaled $105,000 a day. "If you want to get motivated," Jones suggests, "strap that on."

O.K., that was then, and now here's Jones in his splendid office at Valley Ranch in Irving, three Super Bowl trophies always in his line of sight. He's fit and trim (down 60 pounds), a ball of energy at 64, impossibly charming, and when it comes to enthusiasm, a carrier. Things turned out, more or less, even after he fired a legend, got sued by the NFL and kept hiring old Razorbacks to coach the Cowboys. That pitiful team he bought is valued by *Forbes* at $1.2 billion and he has turned that albatross of a stadium into his biggest revenue producer. But what's the fun of this business, really, if your hands aren't shaking?

"Let's go see the stadium," Jones says, and we're off in a black town car to 140 acres of mud in Arlington. This is maybe the final frontier in sports-related architecture. Glass panels 120 feet high will open at each end for autumn breezes, a roof will retract to

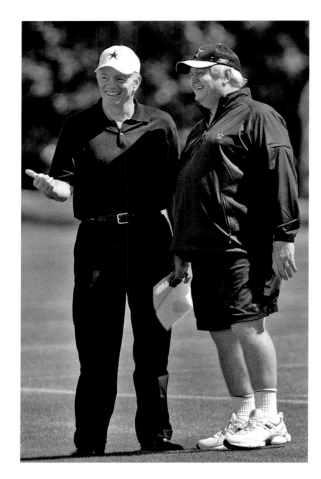

reveal that iconic hole first seen at Texas Stadium, the glass skin will produce a shimmering effect. The place won't be open for business until 2009, but it's undeniably a doozy. Jones did not stint on anything, even when the original cost of $650 million ballooned to $1 billion. The city of Arlington's share was capped at $325 million, meaning that Jones pays for every add-on doodad—such as two 60-yard-wide flat screens hanging over the field—out of his pocket, 100%. "And I'm an adder-oner," he says.

Its glassine luminescence aside, the new stadium will be the biggest in the NFL. It can be configured as needed—normal capacity will be about 80,000, up from 65,529 at Texas Stadium, but fully fitted it will be able to seat more than 100,000 customers.

We meant to say *paying* customers. Because the ability to boost attendance revenues is not so insig-

★ *Jones, the epitome of a hands-on owner, is at home on the field, as all of his coaches, like Wade Phillips, know well.*

TOM FOX/THE DALLAS MORNING NEWS

nificant. When this new facility is finished, it will likely be the most lucrative stadium ever.

The ability to amplify the Cowboys brand, to further exaggerate its already fearsome marketing opportunities, does not argue for parity. Corporate sponsorship in this new stadium is worth more than in, say, Carolina. The Cowboys will profit accordingly without having to spend one more penny on football than the Panthers. So the NFL pretty much lines up small market versus big market, resentments flowing as a consequence. And thus Jones's bid to host the 2011 Super Bowl was not a formality. In fact, the final vote, in May, passed by only 17 for Dallas to 15 for Indianapolis, reflecting more of a grudge than economic sense. A Dallas Super Bowl, just because of the size of this monster, will return upwards of $20 million more to the NFL in ticket revenue alone than an Indy Super Bowl possibly could. Go figure.

"I'M WRITING A one-million-dollar check every day," says Jones, aggrandizing his risk the way any gambler would. "That will keep your eye on the ball."

But there's a kind of fairness at work here. Remember, when Jones came into the league, stadium revenue was an afterthought. That he was able to squeeze some income out of Texas Stadium only speaks to that hand-trembling urgency to pay his bills. He didn't begin selling stadium sponsorships in 1995 to Nike and Pepsi simply to sandbag the NFL (which believed it owned all sponsorship rights); he did it because he needed the dough. After the league conceded, owners no longer thought of their stadiums as rentals but as income streams. And as the owners began to gain control of stadium revenues, the team itself became a kind of loss leader. Sure, there are the national TV contracts, plus attendance and luxury-box income. But is there any easier money than the $30 million-plus contract the Cowboys have with Pepsi? And this new stadium could be the most efficient delivery system for marketing opportunities yet.

Of course, nothing is a sure thing. The NFL is the monster of the moment, its popularity allowing for a tremendous margin of error. Yet this stadium must work for 25 to 30 years to make business sense, and who knows what we'll find entertaining then. Anybody remember horse racing? Boxing?

Jones actually seems to delight in the possibility of failure, however slim it really is. "I'm writing a one-million-dollar check every day," Jones says, aggrandizing his risk the way any gambler would, the way he always has, the tab just higher these days. "That will keep your eye on the ball."

He is mindful that his critics might see a hillbilly pharaoh throwing up his pyramid. He knows it's useless to deny a vanity at work, even if he can't quite acknowledge it himself. "It's healthy," he says, "because it causes you to go the extra mile."

In February, Michael Irvin, an artifact of those glory years, was elected to the Pro Football Hall of Fame. Irvin dumbfounded Jones by asking the owner to present him at the induction ceremony. It makes you wonder about the loneliness of these men at the top when Jones says, "I can count on one hand the times I've been that happy." So Jones threw a party for Irvin, renting the Ghost Bar high atop the W Hotel in downtown Dallas and inviting anybody with any possible link to Cowboys greatness for a night of drinks and snacks. While four cheerleaders danced go-go style and TV screens replayed games from the '90s, alums pressed through the crowd, clacking longnecks with former teammates. Troy Aikman hugged Daryl Johnston, who hugged Emmitt Smith—all remnants of that first, innocent flush of glory. Irvin, predictably late, caused a flash-popping frenzy, even in this crowd. Not many people, you have to admit, can share what they could. Jones just glowed. ★

POSTSCRIPT *The first regular season game played in Cowboys Stadium (as Jones named it—at least until someone could fork up enough to pay for naming rights) was on Sept. 20, 2009. The Cowboys lost to the Giants 33–31 before a crowd of 105,121, the largest in NFL regular-season history. Super Bowl XLV is to be played there in February 2011. If the Cowboys were to make it to that game, it would be their first Super Bowl appearance in 15 years. As of September 2009, the Cowboys franchise was estimated by* Forbes *to be worth $1.65 billion, the most among American sports franchises. And that, of course, does not include the value of Cowboys Stadium itself.*

THE 2000s TEXAS STYLE

★ The yellow-jersey king of the 2000s, Lance Armstrong (born in Dallas in 1971) was named after the Cowboys' speedy receiver, Lance Rentzel.

★ Tony Romo and Jessica Simpson, the controversial Cowboys couple of the decade, split in 2009.

★ Mavericks owner Mark Cuban, showing off his team towel, made the Mavs the envy of the NBA with his lavish locker room.

★ *Tryouts for the hallowed high-kicking squad became a TV reality show in 2006:* Dallas Cowboys Cheerleaders: Making the Team.

Texas native Mike Judge, creator of *King of the Hill*, based the show on personal experience. The fictional setting is Arlen, Texas. Judge once lived in the Dallas suburb of Garland.

★ *A Fox TV hit for most of the decade,* King of the Hill *starred suburban Texas dad Hank Hill, who often lauded his personal hero, Tom Landry.*

★ *PBR world champion bullrider Cody Hart, from Gainesville, Texas, held on for cash at the famed Fort Worth Stockyards in '09.*

THE 2000s IN PICTURES

★ *The Eagles took it on the chin in '09 from the Cowboys and Jason Witten; Dallas won twice in the regular season, once in the playoffs.*
★ *The Cowboys surge of success in '09 was boosted by the flourishing talents of young defensive studs like nosetackle Jay Ratliff.*

★ *Cowboys owner Jerry Jones has never been shy about paying visits to the sideline, or letting the refs know his difference of opinion.*
★ *Bill Parcells, here watching a Terry Glenn sideline catch in '03, spent four seasons trying to make his coaching magic work in Dallas.*

★ Among the Cowboys' greatest offensive linemen ever, Larry Allen was a nearly automatic All-Pro over his 12 seasons in Dallas.
★ Allen's hands, wrapped in battle armor in '03, were, as for any offensive guard, his most vital—and sometimes illegal—weapon.

(FROM LEFT) ROBERT B. STANTON/WIREIMAGE; BILL FRAKES

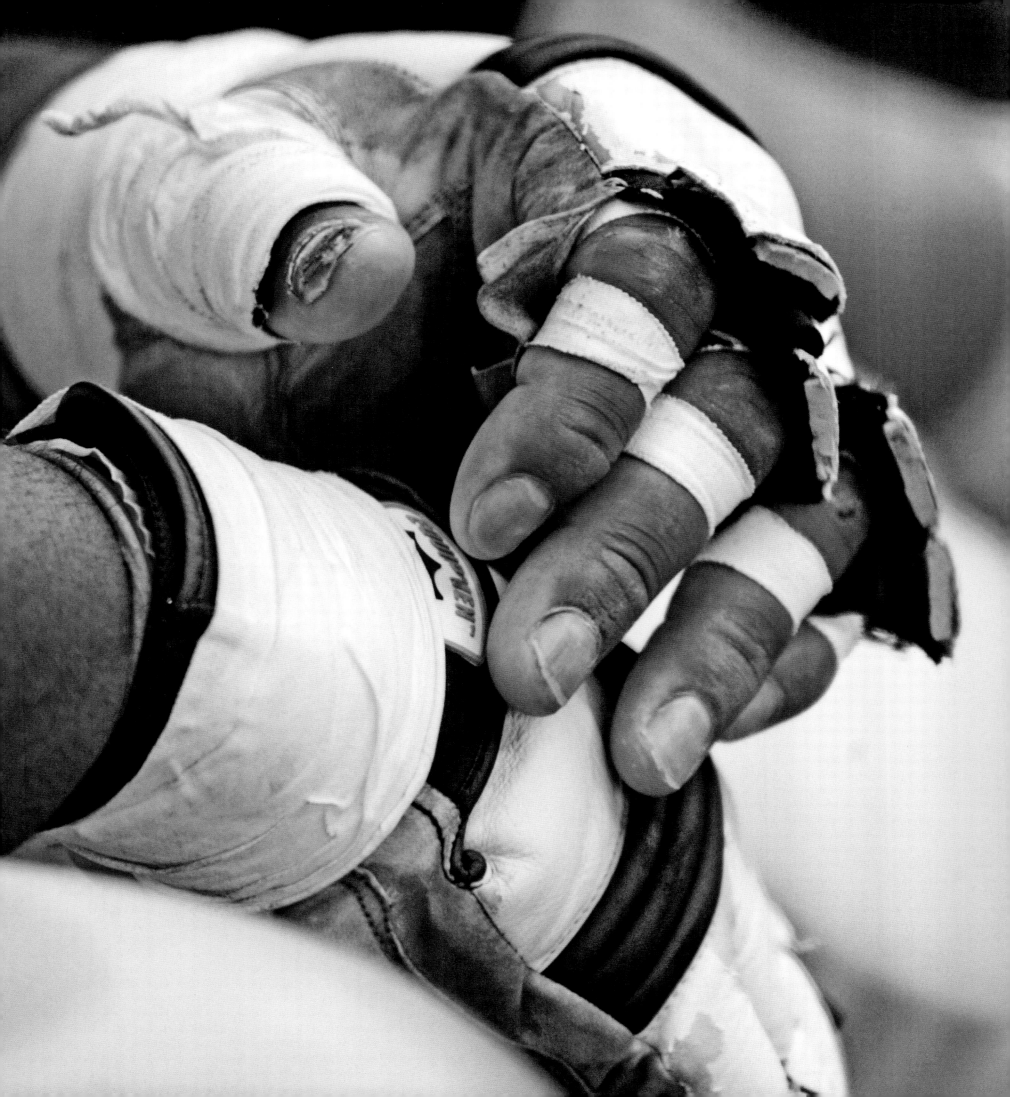

(FROM LEFT) AL TIELEMANS, BOB ROSATO

★ *The revival of the Cowboys' running game in the late 2000s began with the powerful charges delivered by Marion Barber (24).*
★ *Drafted in the first round in 2008, Felix Jones (28) quickly showed the dazzling breakaway ability the Cowboys were hoping for.*

★ Tony Romo's fortunes hit bottom in an '07 playoff game loss to Seattle when he muffed the hold on a late field-goal attempt.
★ Undrafted out of Monmouth College, WR Miles Austin took full advantage of opportunity in '09 and broke out as a full-fledged star.

★ On Oct. 27, 2002, Emmitt Smith set the NFL career rushing record, surpassing the mark of the hallowed Walter Payton.

★ In the uniform of the 1960s, but set to be hero for the next decade, linebacker DeMarcus Ware anchored the Dallas defense.

(FROM LEFT) GREG NELSON, IRWIN THOMPSON/THE DALLAS MORNING NEWS

★ *Part of the Cowboys' image, inseparable from the team itself,*
the Dallas Cowboy Cheerleaders have spent almost 40 years creating a legend.

BILL FRAKES

2000s: The Roundup

★ ALL-DECADE TEAM ★

OFFENSE

QB ★ TONY ROMO (2004–present)

RB ★ MARION BARBER (2005–present)

FB ★ TROY HAMBRICK (2000–03)

WR ★ TERRELL OWENS (2006–08)

WR ★ TERRY GLENN (2003–07)

TE ★ JASON WITTEN (2003–present)

T ★ FLOZELL ADAMS (1998–2009)

G ★ LARRY ALLEN (1994–2005)

C ★ ANDRE GURODE (2002–present)

G ★ LEONARD DAVIS (2007–09)

T ★ SOLOMON PAGE (1999–2002)

K ★ NICK FOLK (2007–09)

RET ★ REGGIE SWINTON (2001–03)

DEFENSE

DE ★ GREG ELLIS (1998–2008)

DT ★ JAY RATLIFF (2005–present)

DT ★ LA'ROI GLOVER (2002–05)

DE ★ MARCUS SPEARS (2005–present)

LB ★ DEMARCUS WARE (2005–present)

LB ★ DAT NGUYEN (1999–2005)

LB ★ BRADIE JAMES (2003–present)

DB ★ ROY WILLIAMS (2002–08)

DB ★ TERENCE NEWMAN (2003–present)

DB ★ ANTHONY HENRY (2005–08)

DB ★ DARREN WOODSON (1992–2003)

P ★ MAT MCBRIAR (2004–present)

COACH ★ BILL PARCELLS (2003–06)

BEST DRAFT SURPRISE

JASON WITTEN TE TENNESSEE ▶
Drafted 3rd round, 2003, 69th overall

Chosen after such tight end luminaries as Bennie Joppru and Teyo Johnson (no, you've never heard of them), Witten emerged as one of his generation's premier players at the position. With six straight Pro Bowl appearances and two 1,000-yard seasons, he is Dallas's career leading tight end in catches and receiving yards.

BIGGEST DRAFT BUST

JACOB ROGERS LT USC
Drafted 2nd round, 2004, 52 overall

A star left tackle for the national champion Trojans, Rogers never adjusted to a switch to the right side of the line necessitated by the presence of all-pro Flozell Adams on the left. Rogers was released early in the 2006 season having appeared only briefly on special teams; he never played an offensive snap for Dallas.

★ A COWBOY TO REMEMBER *Safety George Teague, on Sept. 24, 2000, shoved the 49ers' taunting Terrell Owens as he danced on the Texas Stadium midfield star.*

★ Feeding his ego: In one of the cornier acts in his vast arsenal of post-touchdown celebrations, Terrell Owens grabbed a quick snack.

> BY THE NUMBERS

13 | Cowboys selected for the Pro Bowl following the 2007 season, to set an NFL record for most players from one team.

0 | Uniform numbers retired by the Cowboys through the first 50 years of the franchise. Only four other teams (Baltimore, Houston, Jacksonville and Oakland) have no retired numbers.

5 | Total of top 20 best-selling NFL player jerseys during 2008 belonging to Cowboys. Tony Romo (2nd), Marion Barber (4th), Jason Witten (8th), Terrell Owens (10th) and DeMarcus Ware (20th) represented the Cowboys on NFLShop.com's ranking.

28 | Million dollars won in March 2000 in the Texas lottery by then 47-year-old retired Cowboy Thomas (Hollywood) Henderson. The ex-linebacker said he celebrated his good fortune at his Austin home in his bed with powdered doughnuts, sausage and biscuits, and a glass of milk.

250 | Receiving yards on Oct. 11, 2009 at Kansas City by Miles Austin to break the old franchise-high of 246 set by Bob Hayes against the Redskins in 1966.

AARON GIBSON, JULY 29, 2002
Cowboys offensive lineman, discussing his 410-pound frame:

" **I'm not the first 400-pound player. I'm just the first to admit it.** "

OVERLOOKED GAME OF THE DECADE

OCTOBER 8, 2007 AT BILLS Down 24–16 with just 24 seconds left, Tony Romo, who had thrown five interceptions and lost a fumble, threw a four-yard touchdown pass to Patrick Crayton; but when a two-point conversion pass was stripped from Terrell Owens by Jabari Greer, leaving just 18 seconds, the cause appeared lost. Then lightning struck: an onside kick recovery by tight end Tony Curtis and subsequent 53-yard game-winning Nick Folk field goal as time expired kept Dallas undefeated at 5–0.

WHAT WERE THEY THINKING?

IN APRIL 2008 the Cowboys brass traded two draft picks to the Titans for Adam "Pacman" Jones and then signed the cornerback to a four-year, $13.3-million contract. Jones, with multiple legal run-ins in the past, was serving a league-mandated suspension that had sidelined him for all of '07. Reinstated for '08, he promptly found himself back on the suspended list and in alcohol rehab following an October altercation. Jones was released less than a year after his Dallas career began, having played nine games as a Cowboy.

★ IT'S A FACT: *Emmitt Smith had his worst multi-carry day as a pro in his only game against the Cowboys: six carries for -1 yard as a Cardinal in 2003.*

50 YEARS: The Alltime Team

OFFENSE

QB ★ ROGER STAUBACH (1969–79)
Captain Comeback gets the call over the equally deserving Troy Aikman

RB ★ EMMITT SMITH (1990–2002)
Very few could bump the NFL's seventh-best runner, Tony Dorsett

FB ★ DARYL JOHNSTON (1989–99)
Blue-collar blocker's contributions were integral to Super Bowl success

WR ★ MICHAEL IRVIN (1988–99)
The Playmaker was just too good to leave a spot for the fine Drew Pearson

WR ★ BOB HAYES (1965–74)
The speedy Olympian's thrill factor made him a fan favorite

TE ★ JASON WITTEN (2003–present)
Since '03 only one tight end (alltime leader Tony Gonzalez) has more grabs

T ★ RALPH NEELY (1967–79)
All-Pro right tackle ('67 & '69) moved left to clear a spot for Rayfield Wright

G ★ LARRY ALLEN (1994–2005)
Was chosen to the All-NFL teams of both the 1990s and 2000s

C ★ MARK STEPNOSKI (1989–94, 1999–2001)
Five-time Pro Bowl honoree left after two Super Bowls, returned in '99

G ★ NATE NEWTON (1986–98)
The 6' 3", 320-lb. "Kitchen" was a road-grader in front of Emmitt Smith

T ★ RAYFIELD WRIGHT (1967–79)
Big Cat earned four All-Pro selections and a place in the Hall of Fame

K ★ RAFAEL SEPTIEN (1978–86)
Only Emmitt Smith (986) scored more points than his 874

RET ★ BOB HAYES (1965–74)
His 20.8 punt return average in 1968 is still the highest in the NFL since '61

DEFENSE

DE ★ HARVEY MARTIN (1973–83)
Unofficially ranks as the Cowboys alltime leader with 114 sacks

DT ★ BOB LILLY (1961–74)
Dallas's first-ever draft pick was also the first Cowboy enshrined in Canton

DT ★ RANDY WHITE (1975–88)
Manster was chosen for the All-Pro team each year from 1977 to '85

DE ★ ED JONES (1974–78, '80–89)
Too Tall terrorized QBs with 106 sacks and countless passes knocked down

LB ★ CHUCK HOWLEY (1961–73)
The only Super Bowl MVP from a losing team, he was an elite pass defender

LB ★ DeMARCUS WARE (2005–present)
The lone Cowboy in team history to lead the NFL in sacks, with 20 in 2008.

LB ★ LEE ROY JORDAN (1963–76)
Alabama star became the focal point of the "Doomsday Defense"

DB ★ MEL RENFRO (1964–77)
A Pro Bowl choice in his first 10 seasons, he led the NFL with 10 picks in '69

DB ★ CLIFF HARRIS (1970–79)
Deion Sanders had more pure skills, but iconic Cowboy Harris gets the spot

DB ★ CORNELL GREEN (1962–74)
Ex-cager was first-team All-Pro cornerback by his fifth season of football

DB ★ DARREN WOODSON (1992–2003)
Earned his place here as the franchise's alltime top tackler (1,350)

P ★ DANNY WHITE (1976–88)
Ranks first in punts (610) and second (to Aikman) in touchdown passes (155)

COACH ★ TOM LANDRY (1960–88)
For nearly three decades the man in the hat was the stoic face of the franchise

---

ALL-NUMERAL TEAM ★ THE TOP COWBOY FOR EVERY UNIFORM NUMBER

#	Name	#	Name	#	Name	#	Name	#	Name	#	Name	#	Name
1	Rafael Septien	13	Jerry Rhome	25	Aaron Kyle	40	Bill Bates	55	Lee Roy Jordan	70	Rayfield Wright	85	Kevin Williams
2	Lin Elliott	14	Craig Morton	26	Preston Pearson	41	Charlie Waters	56	Thomas Henderson	71	Mark Tuinei	86	Butch Johnson
3	Steve Walsh	15	Toni Fritsch	27	Mike Gaechter	42	Anthony Henry	57	Vinson Smith	72	Ed Jones	87	Jay Saldi
4	Mike Saxon	16	Steve Pelluer	28	Darren Woodson	43	Cliff Harris	58	Mike Hegman	73	Larry Allen	88	Michael Irvin
5	Clint Stoerner	17	Don Meredith	29	Kenneth Gant	44	Robert Newhouse	59	Dat Nguyen	74	Bob Lilly*	89	Billy Joe DuPree
6	Nick Folk	18	Chris Boniol	30	Dan Reeves	45	Manny Hendrix	60	Don Smerek	75	Jethro Pugh	90	Jay Ratliff
7	Steve Beuerlein	19	Lance Rentzel	31	Benny Barnes	46	Mark Washington	61	Nate Newton	76	Flozell Adams	91	Darren Benson
8	Troy Aikman	20	Mel Renfro	32	Walt Garrison	47	Dextor Clinkscale	62	John Fitzgerald	77	Jim Jeffcoat	92	Tony Tolbert
9	Tony Romo	21	Deion Sanders	33	Tony Dorsett	48	Daryl Johnston	64	Larry Cole	78	John Dutton	93	Peppi Zellner
10	Ron Widby	22	Emmitt Smith	34	Cornell Green	49	Johnny Huggins	65	Andre Gurode	79	Harvey Martin	94	Charles Haley
11	Danny White	23	James Jones	35	Calvin Hill	50	Jerry Tubbs	66	George Andrie	80	Tony Hill	95	Chad Hennings
12	Roger Staubach	24	Everson Walls	36	Vince Albritton	51	Ken Norton	67	Pat Donovan	81	Raghib Ismail	96	Ebenezer Ekuban
				37	James Washington	52	Dave Edwards	68	Herb Scott	82	Jason Witten	97	La'Roi Glover
				38	Ron Francis	53	Mark Stepnoski	69	George Hegamin	83	Golden Richards	98	Greg Ellis
				39	Lousaka Polite	54	Randy White			84	Pettis Norman	99	Hurvin McCormack

*Lilly is the only Cowboy to wear No. 74, and 74 is the only number to be worn by just one Cowboy.

WALTER IOOSS JR.

★ *Despite limited backup QB duty in Super Bowl XII, Danny White sealed the victory with a cheerleader's kiss.*

50 YEARS: The NFL Records

Career Records

★ ALVIN HARPER holds the NFL postseason record for a receiver for highest average gain per reception (minimum 20 receptions) with 27.3 yards per catch. In 10 postseason games Harper had 24 catches for 655 yards.

★ CHARLIE WATERS shares the NFL career postseason record of nine interceptions with Bill Simpson (Rams and Bills) and Ronnie Lott (49ers and Raiders).

★ TROY AIKMAN holds the Super Bowl record for highest career completion percentage (minimum 40 attempts) with 70%.

★ TOM LANDRY's 29 seasons as head coach of the Cowboys places him second in NFL longevity for coaching a single team; he is tied with Curly Lambeau of the Green Bay Packers and is surpassed only by George Halas of the Chicago Bears with 40.

★ LANDRY and the Cowboys' 20 consecutive winning seasons from 1966 to '85 is the NFL record both for a coach and for a team.

★ LANDRY also has the NFL mark for most postseason wins as a head coach with 20, and is tied with Don Shula for the most postseason games coached with 36.

★ THE COWBOYS hold the record for most Super Bowl appearances by a team with eight.

★ THE COWBOYS have been to the postseason 30 times, tying the New York Giants for the most in NFL history (through the 2009 season).

★ THE COWBOYS, in those 30 postseasons, also set the NFL records for most postseason games (58) and postseason wins (33).

★ THE COWBOYS hold the NFL record of nine road playoff wins. (They also hold the record for most road playoff wins in a decade, with six during the 1970s.)

★ THE COWBOYS have been the opponent in the three Super Bowl games with the most turnovers by a team (nine by Buffalo in SB XXVII, eight by Denver in SB XII and seven by Baltimore in SB V).

Emmitt Smith's Records

★ EMMITT SMITH is the NFL's alltime leading rusher with 18,355 yards, 17,162 of which he gained as a Cowboy.

★ SMITH is the NFL's alltime leader in carries with 4,409, 4,052 as a Cowboy.

★ SMITH is the NFL's alltime leader in rushing touchdowns with 164, 153 as a Cowboy.

★ SMITH is the NFL's alltime leader in 100-yard rushing games with 78, 76 as a Cowboy.

★ SMITH holds the records for most postseason rushing yards with 1,586 and rushing touchdowns with 19, all gained as a Cowboy.

★ SMITH holds the record for most Super Bowl touchdowns with five (in three games).

★ SMITH rushed for more than 1,000 yards each season from 1991 to 2001 to surpass the old record of 10 consecutive 1,000-yard seasons co-held by Barry Sanders. Smith is the only player in league history with 11 career 1,000 rushing seasons, consecutive or not.

Season Records and Streaks

★ MICHAEL IRVIN set the record for most 100-yard receiving games in a season with 11 in 1995.

★ IRVIN also holds the NFL record for most consecutive 100-yard receiving games with seven in 1995 (shared with Charley Hennigan of Houston in 1961).

★ DeMARCUS WARE tied the NFL record held by Denver's Simon Fletcher by sacking a quarterback at least once in 10 consecutive games from Dec. 16, 2007 to Oct. 19, 2008.

★ EVERSON WALLS led the league three times in interceptions for a season (1981, '82, '85). No other player has ever led the NFL in interceptions more than twice.

★ THE COWBOYS allowed the league's fewest rushing yards for four consecutive seasons (1966–69) and are the only team to have accomplished that feat.

★ THE COWBOYS have led the league in sacks five times (1966, '68–69, '78, 2008), tied for the most by a team with the Oakland/L.A. Raiders.

★ THE COWBOYS also have the dubious distinction of holding the NFL record for most consecutive home losses with 14 during the 1988 and '89 seasons.

Single Game and Single Play Records

★ THE COWBOYS hold a share of the record (it was matched on three other occasions) for most sacks in a game with 12, a feat Dallas has achieved twice, first in 1966 against the Steelers then repeated against the Oilers in '85.

★ TONY DORSETT holds the record for longest touchdown run with a 99-yard touchdown scamper against the Vikings at the Metrodome in Minnesota on Jan. 3, 1983.

★ LEON LETT holds the record for the longest fumble return in Super Bowl history, an infamous 64-yard runback and fumble (lost inside the one yard line) in Super Bowl XXVII against the Buffalo Bills.

★ *Big-play master Michael Irvin shares his Super Bowl XXVII joy with Alvin Harper (80) and Daryl Johnston.*

50 YEARS: The Lists

Cowboys in the Pro Football Hall of Fame

YEAR INDUCTED

- BOB LILLY ... 1980
- ROGER STAUBACH ... 1985
- TOM LANDRY ... 1990
- TEX SCHRAMM ... 1991
- TONY DORSETT ... 1994
- RANDY WHITE ... 1994
- MEL RENFRO ... 1996
- TROY AIKMAN ... 2006
- RAYFIELD WRIGHT ... 2006
- MICHAEL IRVIN ... 2007
- BOB HAYES ... 2009
- EMMITT SMITH ... 2010

Cowboys' Ring of Honor

- BOB LILLY ... 1975
- DON MEREDITH ... 1976
- DON PERKINS ... 1976
- CHUCK HOWLEY ... 1977
- MEL RENFRO ... 1981
- ROGER STAUBACH ... 1983
- LEE ROY JORDAN ... 1989
- TOM LANDRY ... 1993
- TONY DORSETT ... 1994
- RANDY WHITE ... 1994
- BOB HAYES ... 2001
- TEX SCHRAMM ... 2003
- CLIFF HARRIS ... 2004
- RAYFIELD WRIGHT ... 2004
- TROY AIKMAN ... 2005
- MICHAEL IRVIN ... 2005
- EMMITT SMITH ... 2005

Most Games Played as a Cowboy

- ED (TOO TALL) JONES ... 224
- BILL BATES ... 217
- RANDY WHITE ... 209
- TOM RAFFERTY ... 203
- EMMITT SMITH ... 201
- BOB LILLY ... 196
- MARK TUINEI ... 195
- NATE NEWTON ... 191
- JIM JEFFCOAT ... 188
- LEE ROY JORDAN ... 186
- D.D. LEWIS ... 186

Cowboys Most Often on the Cover of SI (Not Always Main Subject)

- EMMITT SMITH ... 11
- TROY AIKMAN ... 5
- TONY DORSETT ... 3
- GEORGE ANDRIE ... 2
- CHUCK HOWLEY ... 2
- MICHAEL IRVIN ... 2
- BOB LILLY ... 2
- TONY ROMO ... 2
- DEION SANDERS ... 2
- ROGER STAUBACH ... 2
- BARRY SWITZER ... 2
- WILLIE TOWNES ... 2

Record vs. All Opponents 1960–2009

Regular Season

Opponent	G	W	L	T	Dallas win %
Carolina Panthers	9	8	1	0	.889
New York Jets	9	7	2	0	.778
Tampa Bay Buccaneers	12	9	3	0	.750
New England Patriots	10	7	3	0	.700
Seattle Seahawks	12	8	4	0	.667
Kansas City Chiefs	9	6	3	0	.667
San Diego Chargers	9	6	3	0	.667
St. Louis/Phoenix/Arizona Cardinals	84	55	28	1	.663
New Orleans Saints	23	15	8	0	.652
Atlanta Falcons	22	14	8	0	.636
Buffalo Bills	8	5	3	0	.625
Washington Redskins	98	59	37	2	.615
Baltimore/Indianapolis Colts	13	8	5	0	.615
Cincinnati Bengals	10	6	4	0	.600
New York Giants	95	55	38	2	.591
Houston Oilers/Tennessee Titans	12	7	5	0	.583
Chicago Bears	19	11	8	0	.579
Philadelphia Eagles	98	55	43	0	.561
Detroit Lions	20	11	9	0	.550
Green Bay Packers	23	12	11	0	.522
Pittsburgh Steelers	27	14	13	0	.519
Minnesota Vikings	20	10	10	0	.500
Jacksonville Jaguars	4	2	2	0	.500
Houston Texans	2	1	1	0	.500
Los Angeles/St. Louis Rams	21	10	11	0	.476
Cleveland Browns	26	11	15	0	.423
San Francisco 49ers	25	10	14	1	.417
Denver Broncos	10	4	6	0	.400
Oakland/Los Angeles Raiders	10	4	6	0	.400
Miami Dolphins	11	4	7	0	.364
Baltimore Ravens	3	0	3	0	.000

Postseason

Opponent	G	W	L	Dallas win %
Atlanta Falcons	2	2	0	1.000
Buffalo Bills	2	2	0	1.000
Chicago Bears	2	2	0	1.000
Tampa Bay Buccaneers	2	2	0	1.000
Denver Broncos	1	1	0	1.000
Miami Dolphins	1	1	0	1.000
Philadelphia Eagles	4	3	1	.750
San Francisco 49ers	7	5	2	.714
Green Bay Packers	6	4	2	.667
Minnesota Vikings	7	4	3	.571
Detroit Lions	2	1	1	.500
Los Angeles Rams	8	4	4	.500
Pittsburgh Steelers	3	1	2	.333
Cleveland Browns	3	1	2	.333
Carolina Panthers	2	0	2	.000
Washington Redskins	2	0	2	.000
Arizona Cardinals	1	0	1	.000
Baltimore Colts	1	0	1	.000
New York Giants	1	0	1	.000
Seattle Seahawks	1	0	1	.000

Top Ten Nicknames

1. Ed (TOO TALL) Jones
2. Nate (THE KITCHEN) Newton
3. Don (DANDY DON) Meredith
4. "BULLET" Bob Hayes
5. Randy (THE MANSTER) White
6. Thomas (HOLLYWOOD) Henderson
7. Flozell (THE HOTEL) Adams
8. Walt (PUDDIN') Garrison
9. Marion (THE BARBARIAN) Barber
10. Roger (CAPTAIN COMEBACK) Staubach

Top 10 Unlikely Performances

1. RON WIDBY • *84-yard punt, Nov. 3, 1968 at Saints*
2. ALEXANDER WRIGHT • *102-yard kickoff return, Dec. 22, 1991 vs. Falcons*
3. JERRY NORTON • *94-yard return of a missed field goal, Dec. 9, 1962 at Cardinals*
4. TROY HAMBRICK • *189-yard rushing game, Dec. 14, 2003 at Redskins*
5. PAUL PALMER • *Team rushing leader with 446 yards in the 1989 season*
6. AMOS MARSH • *101-yard kickoff return, Sept. 14, 1962 vs. Eagles*
7. JAMES DIXON • *203 yards receiving, Nov. 12, 1989 at Cardinals*
8. ERIC OGBOGU • *3½ sacks in a game, Nov. 25, 2004 vs. Bears*
9. DENNIS MORGAN • *98-yard punt return, Oct. 13, 1974 vs. Cardinals*
10. GARY HOGEBOOM • *389 yards passing, Dec. 22, 1985 at 49ers*

Top 10 Most Memorable Defeats

1. 1-10-82, NFC CHAMPIONSHIP AT 49ERS Montana Stuns Dallas, 28–27 • *Late touchdown catch by Clark ends Cowboys Super Bowl hopes.*
2. 12-31-67, NFL CHAMPIONSHIP AT PACKERS Green Bay Ices Cowboys, 10–6 • *Starr's TD plunge gives Pack title in coldest game ever.*
3. 1-17-71, SUPER BOWL V AT MIAMI O'Brien Boots Cowboys, 16–13 • *Colts kicker ends Dallas title quest with last-second field goal.*
4. 1-6-07, NFC WILD-CARD GAME AT SEAHAWKS Seattle Drops Dallas, 21–20 • *Holder Romo muffs snap on game-tying field goal attempt.*
5. 1-18-76, SUPER BOWL X AT MIAMI Swann is Super, Steelers Down Cowboys, 21–17 • *Receiver needs only four catches to rack up 161 yards.*
6. 1-21-79, SUPER BOWL XIII AT MIAMI Bradshaw Powers Pittsburgh, 35–31 • *QB throws for four scores for third Super Bowl crown.*
7. 11-25-93 VS. DOLPHINS Miami Gets Thanksgiving Gift, 16–14 • *Leon Lett lets win slip away with blunder in freak snowstorm.*
8. 12-30-79 NFC DIVISION PLAYOFF VS. L.A. RAMS Cowboys Fall to Ferragamo, 21–19 • *50-yard TD pass with 2:06 left stuns defending NFC champs.*
9. 11-17-85 VS. BEARS Bears Maul 'Boys at Home, 44–0 • *Ex-Cowboy Ditka hands coach Landry his worst defeat.*
10. 1-15-95 NFC CHAMPIONSHIP AT 49ERS Cowboys Turn Over Crown, 38–28 • *Five Niners takeaways deny Dallas a chance to threepeat.*

★ *In Dallas's first playoff win in 13 years (34–14 over the Eagles on 1/9/10), Miles Austin got a big lift from Flozell Adams.*

Pennants reading:

DALLAS COWBOYS
National Football Conference
5TH ANNUAL SUPER BOWL
MIAMI, FLA.
JAN 17, 1971

DALLAS COWBOYS

★ *The team's first Super Bowl appearance lured all sorts of Cowboy fans to Miami for SB V, a 16–13 loss to the Colts but the beginning of great things.*

ACKNOWLEDGMENTS

★ *A young admirer in Minnesota congratulates Tom Landry after a 20–12 Cowboy playoff win in '71.*

THE LIFESPAN OF SPORTS ILLUSTRATED, BORN IN 1954, ROUGHLY MATCHES THAT OF THE DALLAS COWBOYS. THE STORIES AND PICTURES IN THIS BOOK ARE THE COLLECTED WORK OF THE MANY EXCEPTIONAL SI WRITERS AND PHOTOGRAPHERS WHO HAVE COVERED THE COWBOYS OVER THE PAST FIVE DECADES. THESE PAGES ARE ALSO THE RESULT OF DEDICATED WORK BY CURRENT SI STAFF MEMBERS, INCLUDING GEOFF MICHAUD, DAN LARKIN, BOB THOMPSON, KAREN CARPENTER, STEVE FINE, SCOTT NOVAK, GEORGE WASHINGTON, GEORGE AMORES, SUSAN SZELIGA AND JOY BIRDSONG, AS WELL AS SI GROUP EDITOR TERRY MCDONELL.

PHOTO CREDITS

TABLE OF CONTENTS *(top to bottom from left):* Mark Kauffman, Neil Leifer, John Biever, Walter Iooss Jr., Peter Read Miller, John Biever, Art Shay, George Lange, Fred Kaplan, Joe McNally, Bob Rosato, Carl Iwasaki, Peter Read Miller, Walter Iooss Jr., Peter Read Miller, Bob Rosato

1960s: OPENER *(from left):* Russ Russell/Wireimage.com, Malcolm Emmons/US Presswire, Darryl Norenberg/WireImage.com, Neil Leifer, NFL/WireImage.com, Tim Culek/Wireimage.com, Jerry Cabluck, Vernon Biever/NFL, AP, Tony Tomsic; STYLE *(clockwise from top left):* Courtesy of Dallas Cowboys, Shelly Katz, Everett Collection, Bill Hudson/AP, Dallas State Fair, Tom Kelley/Getty Images, 7-Eleven Inc.; ROUNDUP *(from left):* George Silk/Time Life Pictures/Getty Images, Pro Football Hall Of Fame/WireImage.com

1970s: OPENER *(from left):* Bill Smith/WireImage.com, NFL/WireImage.com, Walter Iooss Jr., John Iacono, Lane Stewart, Walter Iooss Jr., Ross Lewis/WireImage.com, Fred Roe/NFL Photos/Getty Images, Walter Iooss Jr., Manny Rubio/WireImage.com; STYLE *(clockwise from top left):* Alan Band/Keystone/Getty Images, Paramount Pictures/Everett Collection, VCX Ltd./Photofest, ABC

Photo Archives, John Iacono, CBS/Photofest, Al Panzera, Darryl Norenberg/WireImage.com, AP; ROUNDUP *(from left):* USC Athletics, John Iacono

1980s: OPENER *(from left):* Greg Cava, Al Messerschmidt/WireImage.com, Peter Read Miller, Rob Tringali/SportsChrome, John Iacono, Andy Hayt, Heinz Kluetmeier, Peter Read Miller, Walter Iooss Jr., Peter Read Miller; STYLE *(clockwise from top left):* AP, Ronald C. Modra, Universal/Everett Collection, Virginia Sherwood/NBC Newswire/AP, Paramount Pictures/Photofest, Dallas State Fair, Shelly Katz; ROUNDUP *(from left):* AFA Athletics, Mark Perlstein

1990s: OPENER *(from left):* Stephen Dunn/Getty Images, Allen Kee/WireImage.com, John Biever, Peter Read Miller, NFL/WireImage.com, John Biever, Al Tielemans, Mike Powell/Getty Images, Stephen Dunn/Getty Images, Al Tielemans; STYLE *(clockwise from top left):* Robb Kendrick/Aurora Photos, CBS/Photofest, Shelly Katz, D Magazine, Ted Thai/Time Life Pictures/Getty Images, Bill Waugh/AP, Ezra Shaw/Getty Images, Ken Lawdemilk/Fort Worth Star-Telegram/AP, Bob Daemmrich/Corbis; ROUNDUP *(from left):* TCU Athletics, Bill Frakes

2000s: OPENER *(from left);* Aggie Skirball/WireImage.com, James D. Smith/WireImage.com, Greg Nelson, Bob Rosato, Mark J. Rebilas/US Presswire, Glenn James/WireImage.com, James D. Smith/Icon SMI, Greg Nelson, John Biever, Tom DiPace Photography; STYLE *(clockwise from top left):* Jeffrey Lowe, Rondeau/Pressesports, Tim Heitman/US Presswire, David A. Roth, Fox Broadcasting/Photofest, Jonathan Ernst/Reuters; ROUNDUP *(from left):* Mark Humphrey/AP, Mike Thomas/AP

END PAPERS: Team photos courtesy of the Dallas Cowboys

TIME INC. HOME ENTERTAINMENT: Richard Fraiman, Publisher; Steven Sandonato, General Manager; Carol Pittard, Executive Director, Marketing Services; Tom Mifsud, Director, Retail & Special Sales; Peter Harper, Director, New Product Development; Laura Adam, Director, Bookazine Marketing; Joy Butts, Publishing Director, Brand Marketing; Helen Wan, Assistant General Counsel; Anne-Michelle Gallero, Design & Prepress Manager; Susan Chodakiewicz, Book Production Manager; Allison Parker, Associate Brand Manager; Alex Voznesenskiy, Associate Prepress Manager

HEINZ KLUETMEIER

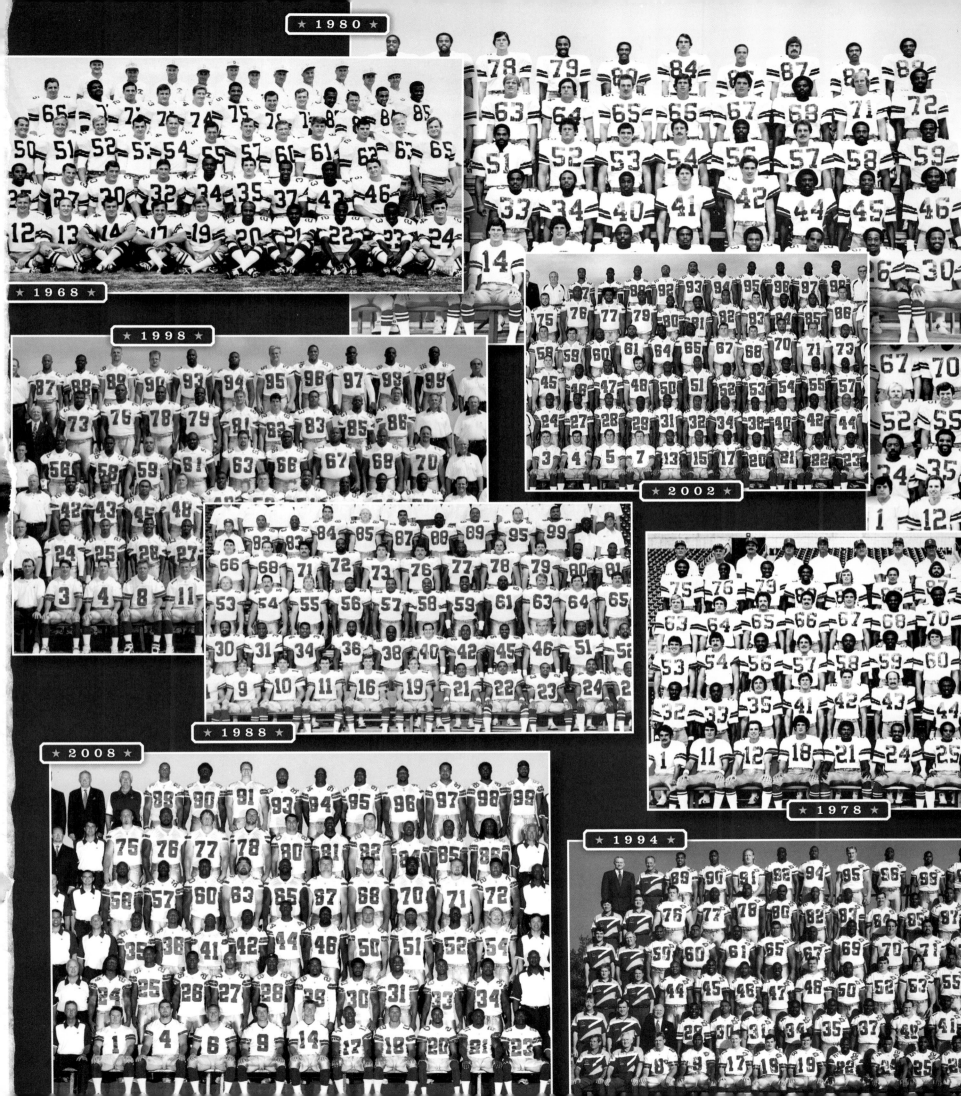

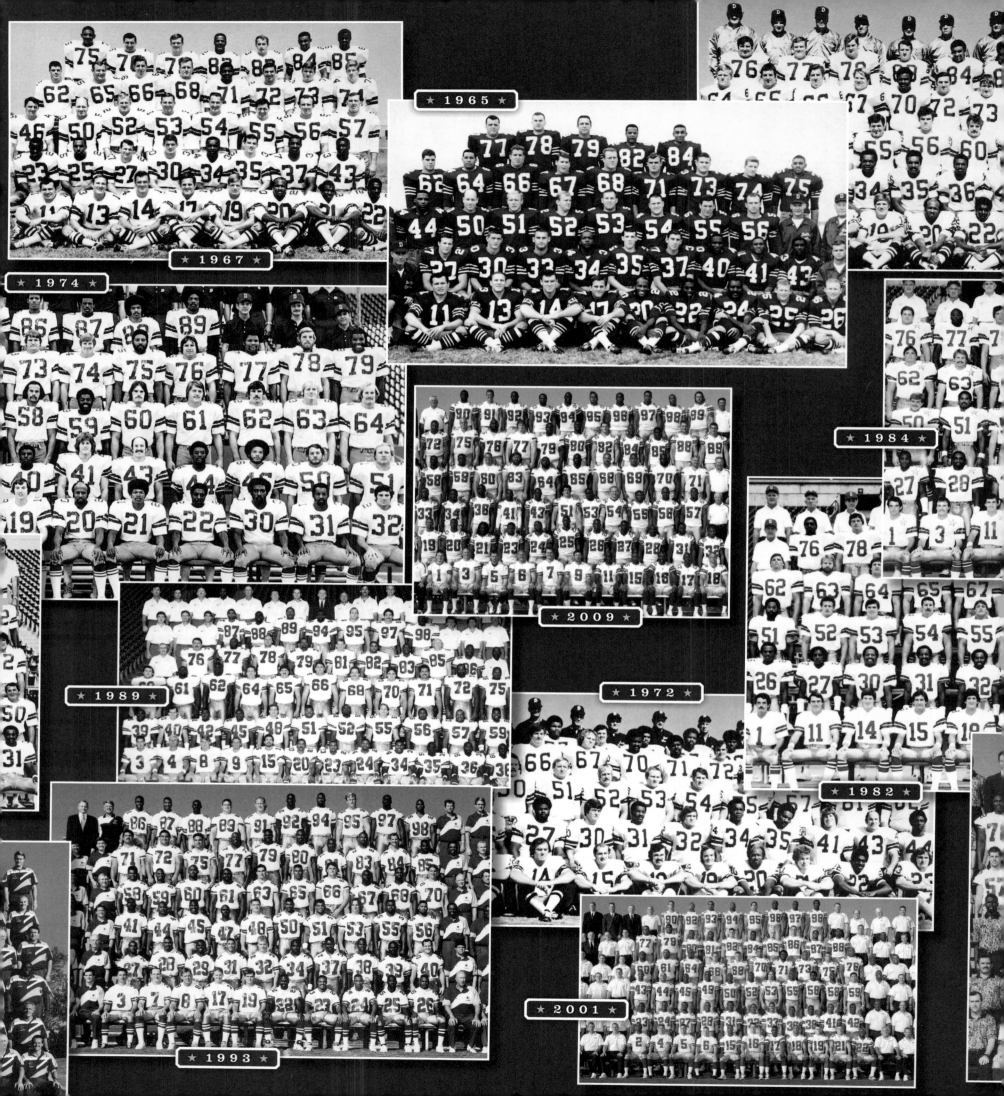